Study of the Lute

Study of the Lute

by Ernst Gottlieb Baron

(1727)

Translated by
Douglas Alton Smith

formerly Instrumenta Antiqua Publications
LuteStuff.com
Raymond Buetens

Copyright ©1976 Instrumenta Antiqua
Second Edition, ©2019 Raymond Buetens

All rights reserved. This book or any portion thereof may not be reproduced or used in any manner whatsoever without the express written permission of the publisher except for the use of brief quotations in a book review.

ISBN: 9781094710662

 Lutestuff.com
P.O. Box 1994
Aptos, CA 95003
USA

Ernst Gottlieb Baron | 1696–1760
Douglas Alton Smith | 1944–
Stanley Buetens | 1934–2009
Book Design | Slub Design (slubdesign.com)

EDITION NOTE:
This edition of the book was completely re-typeset (font: Sabon) and illustrations restored where possible. It had a thorough 21st century proofreading. All text and images from the original are contained in this paperback version. Some images replaced with new scans.

One significant change in this edition is the placement of the original lettered footnotes. All lettered footnotes are now referenced in the Endnotes pages.

FOR MY FATHER

Ernst Gottlieb Baron
Candidatus Juris
J. W. Stör sculp. Norib. 1727.

CONTENTS

EDITOR'S INTRODUCTION I

BIOGRAPHY. VII

ON THE TRANSLATION. IX

PREFACE 5
Most gentle reader!

PART I

CHAPTER I. 18
The Name of the Lute

CHAPTER II 21
The Origin of the Lute

CHAPTER III 25
The Difference Between Various Instruments That Were Also Thought to Be Lutes, and Their Constitution

CHAPTER IV. 34
How Our Lute Came to Italy, and its Subsequent Fate

CHAPTER V 39
The Rediscovery of Our Instrument, and How it Subsequently Came Fromthe Franks to the Germans

CHAPTER VI. 43
The Most Famous Masters of Music Who Lived in Ancient, Medieval, and Modern Times or Who are Still Living, and How They Served Our Instrument

CHAPTER VII 74
The Famous Lute Makers, Their Work, and the True Quality and Virtue of a Lute

PART II

CHAPTER I. 83
The prejudices that are held against the lute

CHAPTER II 109
Genius on the Lute

CHAPTER III 116
The Fundamentals of the Instrument: Posture, Positioning of the Hands, New Tablature, Fingering

CHAPTER IV. 137
The Most Elegant Ornaments [Manieren] on the Lute, Their Designation, Nature, and What is Primarily Important Today

CHAPTER V 144
Playing With Proper Taste

CHAPTER VI. 155
Thoroughbass

SHORT APPENDIX OR DISCOURSE ON THE PROPENSITY FOR MUSIC, VIRTUOSI, AND ALL SORTS OF PREJUDICES 163

ENDNOTES 177

INDEX. 187

PUBLISHER'S NOTE (2ND EDITION) 191

EDITOR'S INTRODUCTION

The *Historisch-Theoretisch und Practische Untersuchung des Instruments der Lauten (Study of the Lute)* of Ernst Gottlieb Baron is the first published attempt at a comprehensive survey of the lute's history. Aside from Baron's book, the Germans appear to have printed no treatise at all on the lute during the Baroque era, a lacuna to which Baron refers in his introduction. German Renaissance lute treatises were brief and were devoted primarily to applied instruction.

Elsewhere on the Continent, as well as in the British Isles, Baroque books on the lute were of a pedagogical nature. The French produced only practical manuals for the lute and theorbo, among them Nicolas Fleury's *Methode pour apprendre facilement à toucher le théorbe sur la basse continuë* (Paris, 1660) and the instructions in Charles Mouton's *Pièces de luth* (circa 1699). English lute treatises from the seventeenth century are Mary Burwell's instructions[1] dating from about 1660, a manuscript source that reflects the teaching of Ennemond Gaultier, and Thomas Mace's *Musick's Monument* (London, 1676), another practical treatise devoted to both the lute and the theorbo, as well as to the viol. Baron's purpose in compiling his *Study* is to enlighten educated non-lutenists about the lute. To this end he covers the gamut of questions pertinent to the subject, as a glance at the table of contents will indicate

---

1. *see* Thurston Dart, "Mary Burwell's Instruction Book for the Lute," *The Galpin Society Journal*, Vol. XI (1958), pp. 3-62.

history of the instrument, composers, lute makers, tablature, ornamentation, thoroughbass, style, and so forth. While the serious modern student of the lute may be disappointed that the author provides only bare introductions to many of these topics and omits many details that would be interesting to know, it should be borne in mind that Baron is deliberately cultivating brevity for the sake of a comprehensive overview.

The first five chapters of Part I, the ancient history of the lute, might be considered Baron's apocrypha, since fact, fable, and fantasy are intermingled. Chapter VI is of interest as a document of eighteenth-century knowledge of and opinions on Renaissance lute music. It is particularly important today, when the Renaissance is often considered the golden age of the lute and the Baroque merely a decadent period of musical decline and too many strings. In this context, Baron's comment on the composers represented in Sebastian Ochsenkuhn's 1558 publication is revealing: "The melodies were still simple and more full-voiced than *cantabile*, but meanwhile we must not scorn these pieces, because simplicity must always precede perfection."

Baron obviously considers the Baroque lute in French tuning with five to seven bass courses to be an improvement over the Renaissance tuning: "Today the lute has been made so easy that even children of seven or eight years can learn something on it." Tablature, too, had become simplified, in his opinion. Baron's remarks on Baroque lutenists are of special importance to us because of his opinions on the style and relative significance of his contemporaries. The most lengthy and frequently quoted section is the one on Sylvius Weiss, whom Baron considers to be the leading lutenist of his time. Although the German Baroque lute school was the direct descendant of the seventeenth-century French lute school, Baron expresses a distaste, perhaps chauvinistically, for Gallic lute music and mannerisms.

The chapter on lute makers is unique. No other lutenist in any period talks at length about specific builders and the quality of their work. Baron's words substantiate what is known from the kinds of instruments that have survived Italian Renaissance lutes by German builders (the Tieffenbrucker family, Hans Frey, Lucas Maler, and others) were highly prized and were rebuilt during the seventeenth century to conform to the new musical style. His remarks on contemporary makers such as Tielke, Hoffmann, and Schelle give us a valuable picture of the esteem that the various seventeenth- and eighteenth-century luthiers enjoyed.

The first chapter of Part II is a polemic against Johann Mattheson, whose biting sarcasm had been directed at the lute in two of his publications. Baron's desire to rebut Mattheson's opinions point by point is directly responsible for the publication of the *Study*.[2]

Two of the chapters in Part II, as well as the Appendix, are of interest from the standpoint not only of music but of sociology and the history of ideas as well. In Chapter IX, Baron stresses the importance of reason, a sound mind, and the power of distinction and judgment for a good musician. These ideas are, of course, characteristic of the Enlightenment. In the Appendix, Baron expresses pietistic views in line with those of the specifically German Enlightenment; he considers

---

2. For a detailed discussion of the controversy see my article, "Baron and Weiss Contra Mattheson: In Defense of the Lute," *Journal of the Lute Society of America*, Vol. VI (1973), pp. 48–62.

an innate skill such as musical talent to be tantamount to a divine calling, carrying with it an obligation to develop it and thereby serve one's fellow man.

In both the Appendix and Chapter III of Part II, Baron treats the subject of proper social behavior and decorum. As a court musician himself, he considers the observance of social amenities when in company and a composed, nonchalant air when performing to be essentials. Consequently, questions of posture and hand position have an expressive significance quite apart from the purely technical aspect of playing the instrument.

Baron also discusses the rhetorical function of music, equating the qualities of a virtuoso musician with those of a good orator. These are: "...the elegance of his words; the loftiness of his thoughts and subjects; and the persuasion and emotion of the affects." Baron's view is in keeping with the eighteenth-century doctrine of the affections. Baron was very well acquainted with the writings of at least two of its chief theorists, Johann Mattheson and Johann Heinichen, and his own university training in law and philosophy gave him a thorough familiarity with classical Latin rhetoricians, to whom he constantly refers.

Finally, the *Study* is a practical treatise as well as a historical and theoretical one. Baron discusses fundamentals of hand position and fingering, explains the system of tablature, and includes a chapter on ornamentation. The last chapter treats the subject of thoroughbass and its application to the lute.

Two foreign terms (for Baron) that appear frequently and that have not been translated in this edition, the French *galant* and the Italian *cantabile,* require some explanation. For

Baron, *galant* seems to have primarily a social and secondarily a musical significance. To be a *galant homme* was to be a man of refined manners, with the well-bred nobleman as the ideal to be emulated, and to be conversant on a wide range of topics in the arts and sciences in other words, to be a man of the Enlightenment. In the first half of the eighteenth century, the light, elegant *style galant* in music began to supersede the more serious Baroque style. *Galant* music emphasized secular, accompanied melody, turning away from fugal counterpoint associated with the Church. A major source of the German predilection for melody was Italian opera, hence Baron's use of the term *cantabile*. The *Study* was Baron's first and most important publication, but it was not his only one. Some three decades after the appearance of his *magnum opus,* he wrote three articles for the *Historisch-critische Beiträge*, edited by F. W. Marpurg. Baron's "*Beitrage zur historisch-theoretischen und practisehen Untersuchung der Lauten*" (in Vol. II, 1756, pages 65–83) is a discussion of the lute's ancient history. The "*Abhandlung von dem Notensystem der Lauten und der Theorbe,*" on pages 119–123 of the same volume, is a defense of lute tablature. In the "*Zufällige Gedanken über verschiedene Materien*" (pages 124–144), "Baron discourses on the duties of a *Kapellmeister*. A separate publication was his brief *Abriss einer Abhandlung von der Melodie* (Berlin, 1756).

Baron also made several translations from the French. The *Essai sur le beau* (1741) of Yves Marie André appeared as *Versuch über das Schöne* in Altenburg in 1757, together with a preface and an appendix, "*Des Herrn Gresset's Rede vom Adel und Nutzen der Music,*" a lecture given in 1751 by J. B. L. Gresset in Paris.

A number of solo and chamber music compositions for

lute by Baron have survived. I have not been able to consult all of the extant manuscripts, so the following will be presented as a provisional list of his works: about twelve solo lute suites; two solo fantasias; several incomplete sonatas and suites for two lutes (only one part survives); three trios for lute, violin, and cello; and two sonatas for lute and flute. Of these, one fantasia was published by Ferdinand Seidel under the title *"12 Menuetten für die Laute samt einer Fantasie von Herrn Baron"* (Leipzig, 1757), and one suite appeared in Georg Philipp Telemann, *Der getreue Musickmeister* (Hamburg, 1728).

Baron's musical compositions are elegant and buoyant, in the spirit of the *style galant*. The solo suites consist primarily of French dance movements, normally the typical allemande, courante, sarabande, and gigue, but always with the addition of one or more movements in the newer style—one or two minuets, a bourrée, air, polonaise, or gavotte—and frequently with a prelude or fantasia preceding the allemande. The suites by Baron are thus quite similar to those of Sylvius Leopold Weiss in form and spirit, but they are not as difficult technically, since Baron tends to remain in first position. The duets and trios of Baron are usually in three movements allegro, adagio, and vivace or presto and are more ambitious than those of earlier composers, for instance the trios of Ferdinand Ignaz Hinterleithner (Vienna, 1699), in which the violin and cello merely double the outer voices of the lute part.

Baron emerges as one of the most important lutenists of the Late Baroque because of his compositions and his long service at the court of Frederick the Great in Berlin (see biography that follows). But his most significant contribution is the *Study of the Lute,* a unique document that records the history and practice of the lute in the words of one of its leading practitioners.

BIOGRAPHY

The following biography of Baron is a paraphrased translation from the two lengthiest sources, both published during his own lifetime. The first part, to 1728, is from Johann G. Walther, *Musikalisches Lexicon* (Leipzig, 1732), and the sequel, written by Baron himself, from F. W. Marpurg's *Historisch-Kritische Beitrage,* Vol. 1 (Berlin, 1754).

Ernst Gottlieb Baron was born in Breslau (now Wroclaw, Poland), East Prussia, on February 17, 1696. He was the son of Michael Baron, a haberdasher and local militia lieutenant, later a sexton, who died in 1717. He was first encouraged to take up his father's occupation, but instead went to the Elizabethanisches Gymnasium (college preparatory school) in Breslau, then left in 1715 for the University of Leipzig, where for four years he attended lectures in the faculties of philosophy and law.

Baron's study of the lute began in about the year 1710 with a Bohemian lutenist named Kohott. After leaving Leipzig, he traveled for a short time to Halle, then visited the courts of Cöthen,[3] Schlaitz, Saalfeld, and Rudelstadt, and finally

---

3. Since this visit occurred in 1719 or 1720, the period of J. S. Bach's tenure as *Kapellmeister* in Cöthen, Baron undoubtedly made the acquaintance of the great master, and we can assume that in all probability Bach heard Baron play. It was customary at that time for a travelling musician of standing to spend some time at the courts he visited and to play for

went to Jena in 1720 for two years. From Jena, he journeyed to Kassel and played for the Landgrave, then to Fulda, spent eight weeks in Würzburg, then traveled through Nuremberg to Regensburg. In Regensburg he met Lord von Reck, the Saxon-Luxembourg envoy, who recommended him to his brother-in-law, Lord Christiani, the Privy Councillor at the Mecklenburg court. From Mecklenburg, Baron returned to Nuremberg, where his book was printed.

On the death of Meusel (a popular lutenist whose first name has not come down to us), Baron was appointed lutenist to the Saxon-Gotha court on May 12, 1728. He remained in Gotha until the death of his sovereign in 1732. Shortly thereafter Baron requested his dismissal, received it, and went to Eisenach, where he was engaged to play with the court chamber and chapel orchestra. Baron remained in Eisenach until 1737, when the improving musical situation in the Brandenburg states moved him to request his release to try his luck in Berlin. The Duke of Eisenach not only assented, but gave him a recommendation to the Crown Prince (later King), Frederick II of Prussia. The Duke assured Baron that if he did not achieve the success he hoped for in Prussia, he could at any time resume his position in Eisenach.

On his way to Prussia, Baron visited and played at the courts of Merseburg, Cöthen, and Zerbst; he finally arrived in Berlin toward the end of 1737. Baron was immediately hired at a good salary as a theorbist, and some years later, on the establishment of a royal chamber and chapel orchestra, he was appointed to it. Because he had no theorbo of

---

the *Kapellmeister* in the hopes of obtaining an audience before the local count or duke and, presumably, a reward for his performance.

his own, Baron received permission to go to Dresden and have one made, but instead he purchased one there from Sylvius Leopold Weiss, the lutenist and theorbist at the court of the Elector of Saxony.

Baron remained the royal Prussian lutenist and theorbist until his death in Berlin on April 12, 1760. Some of his colleagues in Berlin were the flutist J. J. Quantz, the *Kapellmeister*, concertmaster, and composer Carl Heinrich Graun, and C. P. E. Bach.

ON THE TRANSLATION

In this translation I have attempted to transmit the rather quaint style of the original as closely as the gaps of time and language permit. I have pruned occasional redundancies and clarified antecedents to make an English text that will read smoothly and lucidly. Baron wrote in a period when the contemporary national literature was relatively undistinguished and when the German language had no great model of prose to set a high stylistic standard. Hence, if Baron's style seems sometimes inconsistent, jumping from Latin or French eloquence to common German colloquialism, this is not merely characteristic of the author, but of the age. The style of Johann Mattheson, Baron's famous contemporary, is quite similar. Both writers were deliberately cultivating a popular style, as opposed to that of earlier, less readily accessible works on music, particularly those in Latin (for example, Kircher's *Musurgia universalis*).

The original *Study* is without paragraph indentations; those in this translation are editorial. Orthography of names has been normalized to current standard usage (for instance, Johanni Dolando is John Dowland), wherever the name could be identified. I saw no need to translate all of Baron's Latin and French footnote references, since in many cases they were paraphrased in the main text. Editorial footnotes have been added to correct some factual statements of Baron's that have since been proven wrong. I have indicated Baron's footnotes with letter superscripts and my own with Arabic numerals. All of the illustrations are facsimiles, but the transcriptions of tablature in Part II are editorial. This translation is complete, with no omissions of any part of the text.

A translator's task is an exercise in frustration. Often there is no totally satisfactory rendering of a word or phrase, and in this particular case the original is frequently ambiguous. The editorial task was scarcely easier than the translation. Baron was a widely read man, and he enjoyed demonstrating his erudition. To track down and explain every name and reference would have been so time-consuming as to indefinitely delay the appearance of this book, so I have identified only those of primary interest. Nonetheless, I hope that my rendition, however imperfect, of this obstreperous material will help illuminate an unjustly neglected area of music history.

I owe a debt of thanks to several people. First and foremost among these is my friend, lute mentor, and publisher Stanley Buetens, who suggested this project to me in 1972 and who has provided continuous encouragement to help me complete it. Professor William Mahrt of the Department of Music, Stanford University, has offered many helpful suggestions. Michael G. Collins of Stanford's Department of

Classics made almost all of the Latin translations and corrected the often faulty Greek quotations. Professor George Torzsay-Biber of the School of Law, Stanford University, deciphered several passages of medieval and legal Latin. Without the aid of these scholars, this translation would be presented in much less perfect form. The responsibility for any errors remains, of course, my own.

>Douglas Alton Smith
>Palo Alto, California
>June, 1975

Ernst Gottlieb Barons
Candidati Juris,
Historisch-Theoretisch und Practische
Untersuchung
des
Instruments
der Lauten,
Mit Fleiß aufgesetzt und allen rechtschaffenen Liebhabern zum Vergnügen heraus gegeben.

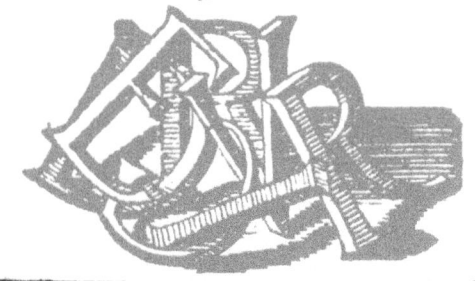

Nürnberg/
bey Johann Friederich Rüdiger.
1727.

Historical, Theoretical, And Practical Study Of The Lute

Prepared with diligence and published for the pleasure of all honest amateurs

by Ernst Gottlieb Baron
(Candidate in Law)

Nuremberg, Johann Friedrich Rüdiger

1727

To His Serene Highness,
Lord Ernst August Duke of Saxony,
Juliers, Cleves and Berg,
also Engern and Westphalia,
Landgrave in Thuringia,
Margrave of Meissen,
princely Duke of Henneberg,
Duke of the March and Ravensberg,
Lord of Ravenstein, etc., etc.

My Most Gracious Prince
and Lord,
resident in Weimar

Most Serene Highness and Gracious Lord:

IN presenting these pages to Your Serene Highness with the most humble gratitude, I hesitate less the more I hope that you may be pleased to look first upon the heart, zeal, and intent before the offering itself, as otherwise in all your doings you demonstrate greatness, and that you will thus imitate God the Highest, who has appointed the kings and princes as his governors on earth.

This sole confidence also allows me the boldness to appear before Your Serene Highness with the present small work and, if it be most graciously allowed, to lay it before your sacred purple robe. In the same manner I hold that it is quite fitting that what is created by the Divine be accepted by the most capable and be preserved and protected until the end of time by the rulers of the earth. Heathen superstition, which once assiduously darkened the true use of mind and reason, had nonetheless appropriated certain trees (quite lifeless and powerless idols) under its control. Since this darkness has disappeared, why should I delay dedicating the laurel of excellent science (as a sign of eternally greening growth) to Your Serene Highness, a Duke who (thank God) is still living and is extremely well-versed in all the fine arts and for whom all staunch muses vie respectfully with one another in building temples and altars in their hearts.

The propensity for good can have no greater reward than to receive approbation from the mouth of one of the wisest, most perfect, and enlightened sovereigns of our time. It is certain that the quest for fine arts and sciences originates in a desire for honor and willing reception and that this desire receives new life through the radiance of royal purple. Thus the musical instrument that has been raised to a high level by eminent persons of nobility and further advanced by worthy artists, but that also has been assailed by irrational precipitance because it is too high for the rabble, seeks refuge with Your Serene Highness in the hope that Your Grace, a magnanimous, august ruler, will not only grant the Horaces and Virgils a benevolent and gracious eye but the Amphions as well. Just as Your Serene Highness has brought about a special respect and love in everyone through earnestness and grace—the best weapons of the Christian princes—Your Grace, the most worthy heir of many excellent virtues of your wise and glorious forefathers, has earned ineffable veneration and amazement not only as a protector of the laws but also as a preserver of scholarship and other fine arts. Since I, as a lover of art, have often had the good fortune to be granted a gracious audience by Your Serene Highness and have since been supported by none other than Your Grace in constancy and unflagging diligence, I would have to be harder and less sensitive than the statue of Memnon if I did not recognize and praise the warming rays of your priceless favor with a clear-sounding tone of gratefulness.

All my thoughts and endeavors have always been directed toward making possible the apparent impossibility of presenting something worthy to your penetrating spirit and intellect. To this end I have found nothing better or finer than to devotedly consecrate the present small work to your most cherished and glorious name, which is able to give my undertaking, weak as it may be, value, glory, honor, dignity, and perfection, and to prefix the same with it.

Formerly proud Rome believed that fortune would be its constant servant as long as the Palladium was preserved within its walls. Although this exaggerated confidence is based upon a heathen blindness, it is nonetheless true beyond doubt that as long as the brilliance of magnificent repute and the luminous grandeur of magnanimous, wise sovereigns holds sway over the fine arts as a strong shelter and unbreakable shield, the arts can expect nothing but elevation. I hope to receive the same from your nobleness and clemency for this insignificant book. It would be my greatest consolation to again obtain your favor, which I presently do not sufficiently deserve, but which I have cause to venerate and preserve as a valuable jewel of my temporal happiness and future undertaking.

May God the Almighty, who watches over kings and princes, uphold Your Serene Highness and your entire Serene Household in future, constant, and everflowering growth and shower Your Grace with the blessing of your immortal, imputrescible, and beloved ancestors so that I, be it near or far, may long have the good fortune to remain with deepest devotion and most submissive respect, as I was long ago and am now with humble ardor, YOUR SERENE HIGHNESS'S AND MOST GRACIOUS SOVEREIGN'S

most submissive and obedient servant,
the author.

Nuremberg
January 12, 1727

PREFACE

Most gentle reader!

THE delicate taste of the contemporary and *galant* world is so singular that a person should pause and consider before burdening it with writings. Yet, despite this, he must not be so quickly discouraged, especially since subjects are often found that have not been examined, but that can nonetheless prove useful and charming to the gentle reader. Although the theological, philosophical, judicial, and medical sciences, in addition to other arts necessary to common life, justifiably and unquestionably have their civic rights that they asserted many hundreds of years ago upon Parnassus, and we might therefore assume that we had almost achieved the truth in most subjects, we still daily find a great amount of things that either are not yet fully understood or, if so, are merely warmed over countless times.

Many people constantly boast of discovering new truths, but when they are examined under the light, these people fare like the Northern and Southern Germans who bicker about who among them invented printing and gunpowder, when in the opinion of learned people both were known in China before the German inventions. Monsieur Huygens long pondered how he might contrive a pendulum clock, but discovered to his distress that another man appeared with one. The opinion of Descartes on the soul of beasts is supposed by others to have been found in the works of a far older Spanish writer, Gomesio Pereira, or even in Diogenes and the Stoics. I will leave what Herr Almeloveen has written about the new way of practicing medicine to the physicians to determine whether or not the basis of his theories is the principles of the Greeks and opinions of other authors, since some accuse him of this.

Since scholars are now competing with one another hourly to get ahead in discovering something new, I hope I do not err in assuming that such a privilege must extend not only to the sciences to which the academicians have dedicated themselves, but also to other fine arts. For everything good, common, and praiseworthy in everyday life deserves to be more clearly and completely examined. Some have done a little too much for the subject and merely fob off the curious reader with odd details, since human reason is insufficient to comprehend the usefulness of such discoveries. But we are nonetheless satisfied with them if we can only quiet our curiosity.

What Monsieur Bordalot's former physician has written to the Duchess of Burgundy about the history of dance and all kinds of physical experiments is only too well known to the learned world. The former he derives from the most ancient times and attempts to assert that it was already in use among the Egyptians, Greeks, and Jews and also had its origin with them. But in his experiments he attempts to prove that we can agitate water with the tone of a flute to such an extent that through its jumping it constitutes a dance. He even goes further and hears music in thunder and the ebb and flow of the sea. Although these writings exist in his brother's name, Bonnet,[a] and are useful merely for an occasional detail or are as useless as Pater Kircher's notation of the song of chickens, cuckoos, and quail, only serving for mere reading and looking; nonetheless these authors have prided themselves on the secrets that they revealed. I will gladly leave them to their delusions. For my part, I have extended curiosity no further than its connection to the main issue, because this small work should serve those who use it not only as a pastime but as a useful tool, so that they might contribute something to art rather than detracting from it.

A variety of writings, among them quite unusual materials, have been treated historically. Even artists themselves have taken matters in hand to distinguish those in the arts whom we have to thank. Who would not extol the industry that Bocheron showed in his dissertation *Sur l'Origine de l'Opera,* in which he attempted to demonstrate how opera gradually arose in France? The work can be found in proof at the Theater of Quinault. Or who would find fault with the Italian sculptor Vasari's zeal for art, or that of Monsieur de Piles, Perault, and others? If the historical, theoretical, and practical examination of the lute, the famous masters and lute makers and other materials belonging to this subject, should earn a small place among these names, that would be the best reward for all my efforts.

There are many amateurs who would like to acquire some initial understanding of this instrument, and they will find it here. However those who only wish to judge the lute without trying their hand will herein have the opportunity to talk about it with considerable justification, as for example Herr Mattheson, who desires the fame of having understood everything exactly and the right to set himself up as a music critic, has done in his *Neu-Eröffnetes Orchestre*. He wrote this work in order to give *galant* people an idea of the entirety of music, a goal that no one will begrudge him, insofar as it has correct truths in it. But since he ventured to hoax these very people with all sorts of distortions and fables, so that they are laughed at by connoisseurs of art, the contrary is proven and the noble truth revealed in Part II, Chapter 1.

There has never been a lack of writings on general topics in the republic of scholars, and if one inspects the large and small volumes written about music, there appear at first to be quite a lot of them. However, most are just as murky as the metaphysics of the beloved ancients. The authors make such a fuss about Greek nomenclature and classifications that I fear all the secrets of music would suddenly be revealed if only the theoretical part were rendered into good German and its essence described according to the rules of logic. Although it also would have been easy for me to add similar hocus-pocus, I have attempted to remove difficulties with clear descriptions and classifications and to judge the subject according to common sense and art.

Why should it not do to bring more clarity to music than has been accomplished with philosophy? To whom are the writings of the illustrious Herr von Leibnitz, of the excellent Privy Councillor Thomasius, and the famous *Hofrat* Wolffen not known? These writers translated all metaphysical technical terms and exorcisms of academic spirits, dangerous as they may have sounded, into the best High German. If it is appropriate in these subjects, which was previously thought unbelievable, why should it not be similarly appropriate in music?

Here others will agree with Jairus, who attended a learned debate at a neighboring university. He heard that some people wanted to reinstate barbarism through the German language, which was fast creeping in. It will serve to answer Jairus and others that beautiful and *galant* music is no more bound to Greek designations than true scholarship is to Latin.

The merry French nation has always attempted to pay homage to those who have made high achievements in the arts, no matter what their nature, because they consider that the honor of the entire nation is based upon having many talented people, and they err all the less the more their zeal for brave artists is applauded. They have long collected famous poets and musicians, and Herr von Tillet[b] has built himself an immortal memorial among art lovers with the *Monument* that he composed for the poets and musicians of his country.

Although I cannot accomplish this with as much splendor as he did, and in addition the precious metal and other expensive things are lacking, the reader should still be content that I, too, have undertaken to liberate great people and fine artists from oblivion. When scholars of all times have carefully recorded the particular merits of those they have personally known, why should not a history of musicians or other artists be written for the pleasure and enjoyment of posterity? The appendix on propensity for music, virtuosi, and other prejudices that occurred to me is for the purpose of educating those (excepting rational connoisseurs) who in the indicated circumstances tend to exercise their eagerness and curiosity more than their good judgment.

Everything appearing in the entire book is either historical or artistic. As for the former, I have relied upon the sources themselves; but all that pertains to art is treated theoretically and practically. I have based the theory upon principles derived from the nature of the subject itself, so that these remain invariable. Practice, on the contrary, I take from the examples of famous people, and I give instructions for using the writings of fine artists.

Originally, I was unwilling to make public a thing that I had compiled for my own amusement, but since many of my good friends and fine connoisseurs of art encouraged me to do it, I finally could no longer refuse to see whether such a subject might not be of interest to the public. Thus, if this work and love of art may have the good fortune of pleasing its readers and music connoisseurs, I will attempt from time to time to contribute more and correct those errors that may perhaps have occurred because of shortness of time and because I am constantly traveling.

Yet I can almost predict how many a Zoilus will turn up his nose at me and gnash his teeth, but here I can do no more than use as a pretext the example of Christopher Columbus, the Spanish admiral and discoverer of the New World, and the egg that he stood on end. I am aware that many people are contemptuous of Plato and Aristotle and other good people only in order to be looked upon by everyone as genuine philosophers themselves. If God and fortune grant more leisurely circumstances, then I can introduce whatever does not please Momus, even if he is right. My consolation is that it is easier to find fault than to do or discover something oneself.

In the meantime, I wish the wise reader well; and may he judge these pages according to probability and the principles of truth. He may rest assured that this undertaking has been for no other reason than to please worthy amateurs. I consequently anticipate a kind reception and commend myself to his further benevolence.

To my friend the author

What Herr Baron teaches us here about his lute
Is the least that has made him famous.
Many princes know, and Silesia admires
That he has here achieved so much before thousands.
Not enough: he imitates Virgil, Horace and Homer
And to be brief, the great [Caspar David] Lohenstein.
Can Silesia bestow upon us anything nobler
That might bring Germany fame among foreigners?
No, no! We see in him Amphion, Jubal, Zethen
And what once graced Epaminond in Thebes.
Antigenides extols him, the poets praise him.
He has studied Pythagoras and the Stagirite.
To be sure, a Momus will prattle a lot with antitheses
And Nisa will perhaps even be touched by Mopsus.
Yet Herr Baron considers all this to be distortions.
If he be, then art and science are despised.
The fact remains (I'll say it most truly!),
Whoever has not his spirit, whoever loves no Muses
Should not tread too near to either
For one gives no pearls of wisdom to Davus.*
What is divine** in itself, in origin, and nature,
What pleases princes and even comforts envy

---

* Quintilian. *"Quis ignorat Musicam tantum illis jam antiquis temporibus non studii modo, verum etiam venerationis habuisse, ut üsdem Musici, et Vates, et Sapientes indicarent ur;"* Ac Isidor. Etymol. *"Itaque sine Musica nulla disciplina potest esse perfecta, nihil enim est sine ila."*

** *"Origo sane ejus Coelestis memoratur, ipsiusque ratione Mundum esse compositum, imo adhuc Coelos harmonice moveri testantur."* Horat. & Beroald. in Qu. Tusc. item Cic. in Somn. Seip. & Macrob. 2. ibid.

May be read in Baron's hand and in his book,
In spite of anyone (how could it be?) who represses him.
Good luck for honor and victory, good luck for laurel blooms
That Fortuna places on him and Pallas strews.
May his vegetation be ever green, his weal brazen and firm,
As long as strings and art stir on Pindus' heights![1]

Christoph Augustus Laemmermann, J[uris] V[triusque] D[octor] and Attorney at Law in Nuremberg

---

[1]. It was common in the seventeenth and eighteenth centuries for the author or publisher of a book to ask a friend to write a panegyric in honor of the author and his new work. This poem by Laemmermann, presumably a lawyer acquaintance of Baron's, is composed in doggerel and does not merit the effort of a rhymed translation.

PART I

Introduction to the Historical Section

ALTHOUGH the matter upon which I am venturing is somewhat thorny, partly because of the difficulty of completing what is begun, and partly because of its uncertainty with respect to history, surely no one can hold it against me if I undertake to break the ice systematically and submit the learning that belongs to our splendid instrument, so that others can follow more spiritedly. Someone must always make a beginning. Therefore Aristotle was not discouraged from being the first to systematize his philosophy, although he immediately thereafter had many devotees and enemies. Various famous men have appeared and written one thing or another about musical instruments. There is for example Franchino Gafurius' *De harmonia musicorum instrumentorum*, a treatise that he published in Milan; Berno Abbas Auginensis published *De musica et instrumentis musicis;* and the admirable Michael Praetorius published the treatise *De organographia* himself in Wolfenbüttel in 1619.

This learned and industrious man [Praetorius] was concerned not only with those types indigenous to Germany; the fire that drove him to the elaboration of such a rare and splendid work brought him to the point of also examining everything in the nature of each instrument of ancient and modern times in foreign and even barbaric nations. He even examined the vulgar instruments that are used only by peasants and the most simple people, and discovered types that were quite unknown to us at the time.

Although, to be sure, these famous writings contain an enormous amount of good information, it is nonetheless very general in nature. In addition, the abovementioned people lived in times when the cultivation of our noble instrument was still in a rather poor state. Salomon von Til, who was Professor and Servant of the Divine Word at Leiden, earned great respect among the lovers of musical antiquities with his book on the art of poetry, singing, and playing, but what he wrote serves only historical understanding. However, those who have always been considered by the refined world to be great masters have distinguished themselves more with musical compositions than with other writings that lead to true understanding. Everyone who has even a little knowledge of our instrument will be aware of the endeavors of Mouton, Gallot, Gaultier, Saint Luc, Philipp Franz le Sage de Richée, and so forth, and although they took great pains, they have still done nothing more than place their French lute pieces before the eyes of the world, either in copper engravings or in manuscripts.

Some famous masters in Germany, as well as in Vienna, Prague, and elsewhere, have endeavored to do all that was possible for the improvement of our instrument. But no one has yet determined to illuminate the whole pedagogy with the light of healthy reason and to look upon it with philosophical eyes in the interest of historical as well as artistic understanding. Thus learned, curious enthusiasts and beginners would gain more insight and be freed of many prejudices. The learned ones will, I hope, greet such a book with enthusiasm, for the literature has always been deficient in such matters. To that end I have included in this work a variety of detailed information that contributes to a thorough understanding. Without knowing this, no scholar, insofar as I consider him also a *galant homme,* can pass muster, because the chief attribute of a scholar is his ability to discern not only in matters of theology, jurisprudence, medicine, and so forth, but also in the other noble arts that serve to adorn the remaining faculties. Thereby the concept that many a person forms of a subject might not come out so downright asinine, as I have, unfortunately, often had to experience.

In addition, the lute has earned a special reputation among the greatest and most qualified persons, so that according to Praetorius' description it is a truly ennobled instrument. It has risen through German skill to such perfection that one can almost say it could not be brought further. However, because I have now and then, as the above reasons show, met with deficiencies both in the works that treat the subject and in the unconsidered judgments of people, and have myself attempted, as far as possible, to assess the worth of the subject, I have therefore endeavored to speak more about this curious subject. For my part, I wish no more than to complete this project, whereby I have all good intentions, for the pleasure and use of all worthy amateurs.

CHAPTER I

The Name of the Lute

THE best order is to proceed from the name to the subject itself. Therefore I will dwell upon it, so that the reader may know where various learned people believe our instrument got its name. Sebastian Ochsenkuhn, who served as court lutenist to Elector Otto Heinrich of the Palatinate in 1558,[2] asserts in his published book that the lute, which in his day was called *leutum* by the Italians, received its name *a levore* or *levitato*. This was namely, as he says, "from its light weight, or that it is simply furnished and not heavy to carry, and can easily be toted around," and that it was originally entitled *levitum* and then *leutum* by leaving out the letter *i*.

Joseph Scaliger and Bochart us derive the name from an Arabic word *allaud*, which the learned Society of Trevoux included in its great lexicon. Although this designation is a bit too far-fetched, Herr Nehring nonetheless joined its camp in his historical, political, and juridicial lexicon, in which he similarly asserts that the word *lute* stems from an Arabic word *ud*, which is supposed to mean a lute, and says that the Europeans merely kept the article *al* or *el* as a prefix. Herr Hübner is of the opinion that the origin of the designation is Germany. He says: "The Italians took

---

2. Sebastian Ochsenkuhn (1521—1574)

our German word *lauten* (to sound) and called the musical instrument (which is called *chelys* or *testudo* in Latin) *liuto*." Now I admit that Herr Hübner's opinion on this matter could very well be possible. But in all probability this explanation is a bit too obscure, since it is certain that our beloved instrument was in vogue earlier with the Italians, who were also cultivated earlier than the Germans, and they will not have lacked a name for it.

I also think, but not conclusively, that in such matters one must consider the order of the times, as gradually one nation after another bursts out of the darkness of ignorance and the *galant* sciences come into the bright light. We must credit the Italians, since the fifth century, for searching out everything pertaining to instruments and to music from the ruins. We will hear more about this below from Boethius.

Therefore we shall not err in searching for the name in the object itself, and attaching the designation to the instrument as its nature demands. Jean Baptiste Besard, in the *Thesaurus Harmonicus* he published for the once famous Laurencini, a Roman knight, makes a very clever deduction and derives the word *Laute* from *la* and *ut*, or from the beginning and end of the hexachord. For it is known that our beloved predecessors in this noble art included all of music in the syllables ut, re, mi, fa, sol, and la, which have their origin in a hymn to Saint John.[c] Now no one will dispute that our noble instrument, together with the keyboard, is one of the most full-voiced and perfect instruments and could thus best share this derivation of the name, because it best corresponds to the lute's natural character and perfection.

For my part, I do not wish to start an imperial war over

the case. It is sufficient that everyone know the thoughts of each of these men. However, all cultivated nations in which our instrument is known call it by different names, which, as one can see from their similarity, have the same origin, thus it will not be inexpedient to add these at the end and report that the French call it *lut* or *luth*, the Spaniards *laud* or *laut*, but the Italians *liuto*. I hope therefore to have furnished whatever information exists about the name, *quia ultra posse nemo obligatur*.[3]

---

3. Because it is incumbent upon no one to attempt anything besides.

CHAPTER II

The Origin of the Lute

To report anything certain about the lute's true origin seems as difficult as counting the sands on the seashore. If there were someone who had something demonstrative on the subject, I should not find it difficult to exclaim with Horace: "*Nil desperandum Teucro Duce et auspice Teucro.*"[4] We must accept information as we find it. Therefore the abovementioned Salomon von Til is correct when he earnestly complains:

> Here in the beginning I hear a general complaint from science, whereby it especially accuses the poets of carelessness, for they, in order to create their verses, have mixed up many names and mingled the stringed instruments of Mercury and Apollo with such confused designations that some people find themselves in a labyrinth. Thus, we find the names *chelys*, *lyra* and *cithara* mistaken by them for like-sounding instruments and confused. Thereby, in the course of time, an abominable ignorance creeps into music, together with confusion of objects and names, since the old names have been applied to completely different instruments. This can be seen in the instruments that are known today by the names of *leyer* and *cithar*, but by their form they have nothing in common with the old ones. (p. 74 & 75, etc.)

---

[4]. "Nothing is to be despaired of, given the leadership and protection of Teucer."

Julius Caesar Scaliger, in the fifteen books that he wrote disputing the *De subtilitate* of Hieronymus Cardanus, charges Cardanus with bringing more confusion than truth to the light of day with his examination of instruments.[d] To make distinctions in such matters, we must differentiate between Mercury's and Apollo's inventions. We should find the matter easier if we consider that the latter invention had its origin in the bow of Apollo's sister, as is maintained by an unknown writer whose incomplete work is considered an appendix to Censorinus. According to the story, he says: Apollo noticed the loveliness of the sound of his sister's bow and the agreement of the tunings and forthwith strung up a harp. He noticed that the most tightly strung strings awakened the brightest tone, and those strung somewhat looser made lower tones. From that he ventured to make the three hexachords. Thereafter he ceded the instrument to Linus (who is considered a son of Apollo and the nymph Psamate), and the latter left it to Chrysostemis upon his death.[e] Now if this is true, we would in all probability have to name Apollo the inventor of the so-called harp of David.

The instrument that the Greeks say Mercury invented (and which was actually called the lyre of Mercury) is also called *chelys*, and, by the poet Propertius and Festus Avienus,[f] *lyra testudinea* or tortoise-shaped lyre. The learned and excellent scholar Scaliger, who was the first to attempt to distinguish Apollo's instrument from Mercury's (in his *Notis ad Manlinum*), explains a passage in Homer's "Hymn to Mercury" (verses 47 to 51).[g] Mercury found a dead tortoise and made from it an instrument or toy. After he had put arms on it and connected them with a crossbar, then attached crossribs and added a soundboard underneath, and strung it with seven strings, he then played merrily upon it.

The site of this invention is revealed to us in the following manner by the famous writer Servius, who explains the poetic secrets of Virgil: Once when the Nile River returned to its banks, it had left different kinds of animals lying upon the land. Thus a tortoise remained, its flesh decayed, with nerves left stretched in the shell. When Mercury plucked it, it produced a sound from whose imitation the lute, or incorrectly, the *cithar*, was born.[h]

From this it is obvious that our instrument has its origin in Egypt. Even Jamblichus' *de mysterüs Aegyptorum* refers to all Egyptian writers who consider Mercury to be the restorer of all sciences after the Flood.[i] Horace was also bold enough to name him the father of the curved lyre.[j]

The excellent and learned Herr Otto Sperling, who explains the medal of Empress Furia Sabina Tranquillina, Gordiani's wife, with very learned remarks,[k] extracted the figure of this instrument from the coins of Nero and Trajan and left it to us as a faithful remembrance, as can be seen here:

The fact that only four strings can be seen on it must perhaps be due to carelessness on the part of those who stamped the coin, for such things often happen today as well, when painters and sculptors make something after their own fantasy and have no real idea of the proper parts of an instrument.

It is enough for us to know that this hollow turtle gradually became the body of a lute, as we will want to recall from time to time below when we consider its changes, especially under the Romans. For now, however, we can be content to have observed this very dubious matter in its earliest and most extreme simplicity.

CHAPTER III

The Difference Between Various Instruments That Were Also Thought to Be Lutes, and Their Constitution

THE poets and writers give us many names that others consider to be lutes without any differentiation, so that Salomon von Til was moved to write: "To attain a better understanding of this stringed instrument, it will be necessary to examine its various forms. Understanding begins with the various names that have been given to each special instrument as a differentiation." (p. 74, par. 3.)

Monsieur Longepierre, too, in his remarks on Anacreon, cites various families of stringed instruments that convince him that because of a difference in the name, there must also be a difference in the thing itself.[1]

For the present, our task is not to examine how the other instruments he cites were different from our lute, but rather to consider those about which there have been suspicions, or that were clearly thought to be lutes.

So as not to depart from sequence, I will examine early writers' various opinions on this matter as best I can, so that we can see the reasons more clearly. The first to come to my attention is Clemens Alexandrinus, who holds opinions about the lyre that had been disproven by much earlier writers than he. From this we can see that he must have understood little about music and its instruments, although he thought highly of it, for he counts the lyre among the instruments that made soldiers desire to fight, as the trumpeters and military drummers do today, and says that primarily the Cretans had used it to this end.[m] However, he contradicts himself immediately, saying that the Greeks used it at feasts and other festive occasions.[n] Now this instrument cannot possibly have made such a terrible tumult and din that it would have roused an entire army to murder and mayhem, although I admit it was more appropriate in social company, since it goes well with the merriment of glasses. This cannot be presumed either of Apollo's invention or of Mercury's *lyra testudinea*, from which all other kinds of lyres originated. It would be equally nonsensical to undertake such a thing with a lute, harp, or cittern, since the ancients knew nothing of brass or steel strings, but were wont to string their instruments with twisted silk thread, or at the most sheep gut, as Homer[o] and Pollux[p] say.

So that the false basis of Clemens Alexandrinus' opinion may become more obvious, I have illustrated here all kinds of figures as found on coins and old marbles.

APOLLO CVM LYRA EX STATVA ANT.
MARM. PVLCHER. OPERIS. ROMAE AP.
PRINC. JVSTINIANI.

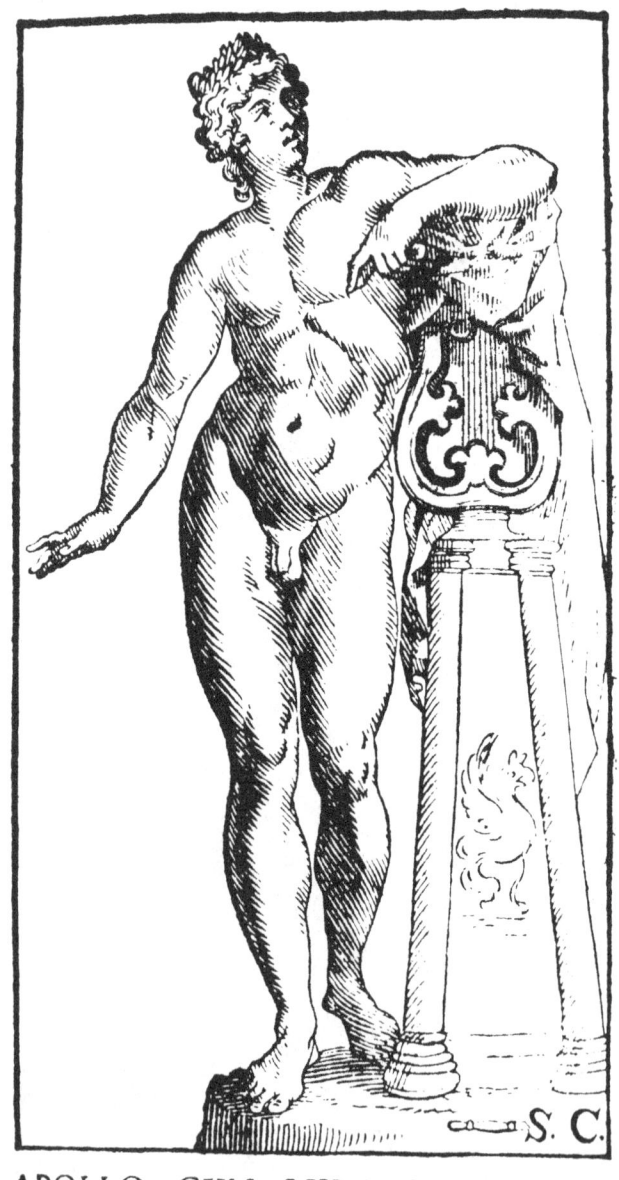

APOLLO CVM LYRA EX STATVA
ANTIQVA QVAE EXTAT ROMAE.

29

30

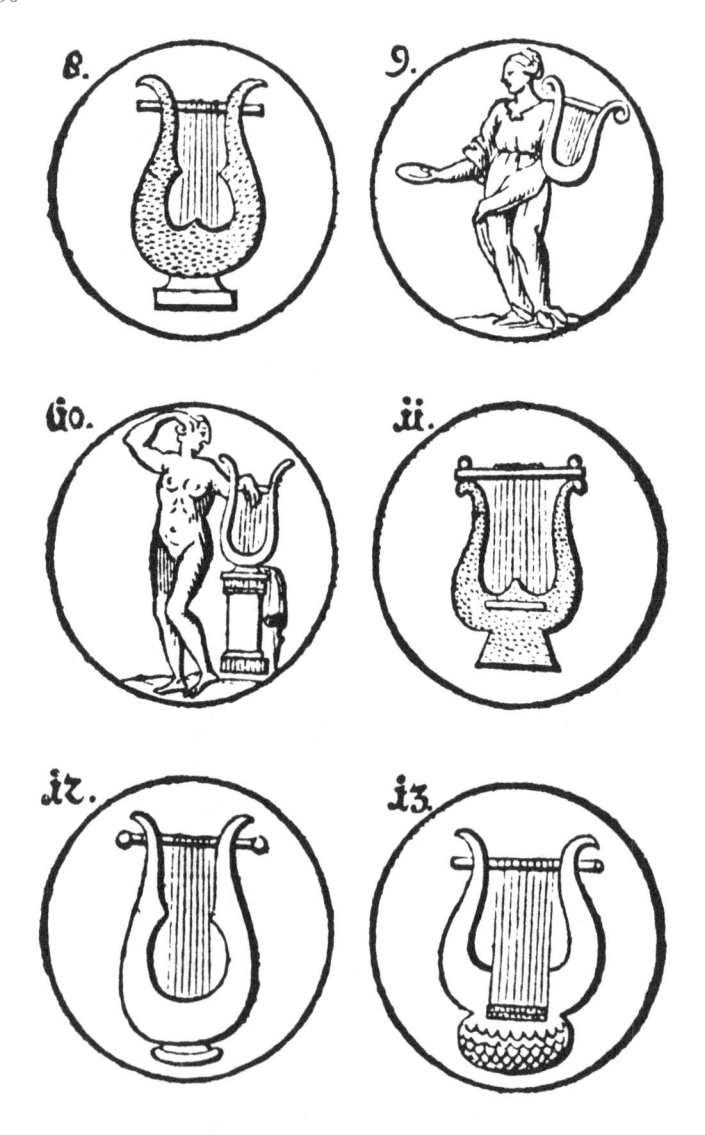

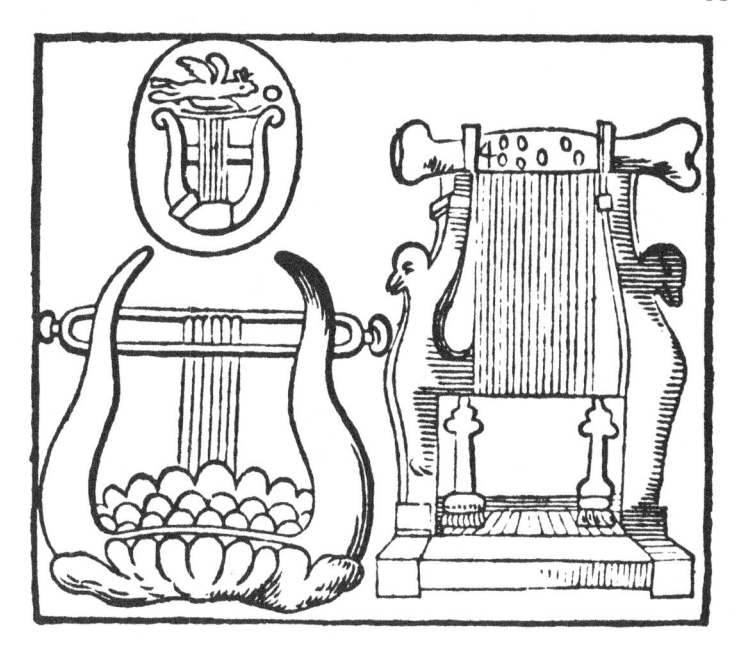

The coins of Nero, upon which the nude figure of Apollo can generally be seen, the Greek coins, and especially those of Megara, the Emperor Caracalla, of Calcedonia, of the Empress Furia Sabina Tranquillina, those of Cos, the Emperor Antonius Pius, and Gallienius, and the Perinthiers give us the best opportunity to visualize the subject. We can thus certainly believe that if all these lyres were put together they would not produce the tremendous noise Clemens imagined. From this we can also see how false it is to call them *testudines* or lutes, since their origin was completely different from the *lyra testudinea*.

The famous Greek poet Anacreon recalls an instrument that he calls *barbiton*, which Monsieur Longepierre considers a lute but Madame Dacier thinks is a guitar. Longepierre maintains that he only used the word *luth* in the translation so that it would be understood, but Dacier cannot help herself and makes a complete mishmash of his thoughts. Thus it will be best to hear Anacreon himself.[q] He says he wanted to go and play his *barbiton,* not that he wished to have the honor of winning the prize in the contest, but rather at this time (when he lived) those people whose erudition, refinement, and wisdom had risen to the highest peak of perfection were playing it. He even says that this instrument, which he here calls *kithara* and is taken to be synonymous (which happens quite often), was consecrated to Apollo along with the laurel tree and the sacred tripod.

From this we can see that the instrument was held in particular esteem by the Greeks, as the assertion of Anacreon testifies.[r] The Greeks attribute its invention to Terpander, who was born in Lesbos, and I believe that the Latin poet Horace must have meant this Terpander in his "Ode XXXII."[s] Although these are the facts of the case, we still cannot call it a lute. For my part, I would sooner think that it was a fiddle or a kind of violin, and it must have gotten its name from the Persian word *barbat* [بربط], particularly since Goilus ascribes a violin to it, as can be seen here.

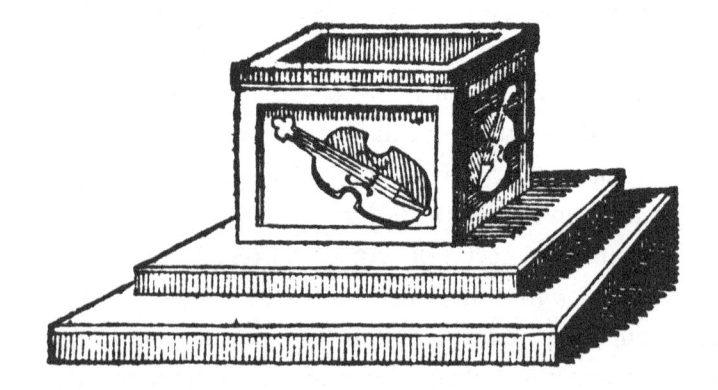

Therefore we can see that it looks much more like a violin, which was also used by the Orientals. Because this instrument was known to the Persians, we have cause to trace the origin of today's violin to it.

Horace, who composed "Ode XXXII" in honor of his lyre, calls it *barbiton* as well as *testudinem* in these verses. We should not, however, be particularly troubled by this, because a general complaint of scholars is that the ancient writers confused these instruments so much. To prove this even more, we only have to open Book Three of Isidore's *de orig.* to find that he uses the word *organum* (by which we today understand an organ) for all stringed instruments.[t] In Books Two and Five, Lucretius even names *citharados the organicos,* but Juvenal, in "Satire VI," called *citharas* the *organa.*

The ancients made their instruments extremely costly. There is information that they ornamented them with gold, silver, *electro,* which was a kind of mixed precious metal, and even with golden rings and all kinds of precious stones. Authors who treat the subject of stringing, and scholars of today as well, are in disagreement about it. I prefer to believe that the ancients strung their instruments as they pleased, as we see even today that the lute has eleven, twelve, thirteen to fourteen courses or more, although it is still the same instrument. I will pass over other stringings for now.

I do not want to dwell upon this material further, for I think it is time to consider how our noble instrument came to the Romans. In the meantime, everyone can believe what he wishes about it, because I will not venture to press my opinion upon anyone.

CHAPTER IV

How Our Lute Came to Italy, and its Subsequent Fate

We have previously observed the origin of our noble instrument and its state of extreme simplicity under the Egyptians and Greeks. Now we turn our eyes and disposition to the Occident and witness the manner in which it came from the borders of Asia into magnificent and charming Italy. I think that it would be most suitable to consider the chief transformations in the whole Roman Empire, whereby not merely external customs, which were formerly founded upon a sedate earnestness and strict virtue, but even arts and sciences changed totally in the public regard. The year 568, after the building of the city of Rome, when Spurius, Poshumius, Albinus, and Quintus Martius Philippus were mayors, not only cheered the Roman people with a new and splendid victory as Cnejus Manlius Volso triumphed over the Galatians in Asia, but also introduced completely new customs that were far removed from the old earnestness. The mischief that Volso had allowed his army while it was still in Asia made the soldiers remember afterwards the merry cities of Asia more than their previous valor, and they strove to imitate the amorousness of that land as well as its extraordinary wealth and splendor when they arrived home again. Therefore Titus Livius was moved to bemoan this situation and the lascivious transformation of the Roman people and to tell us at the same time what kinds of treasure and strange arts the Romans brought from Asia in those days.[11]

For when they returned, their countrymen saw magnificent beds with all sorts of metal inlay, splendid bedspreads, exquisite carpets, curtains, woven cloths, reckoning slates, and buffets that had in those days been considered the most magnificent household effects. And furthermore, harps, lutes, and all kinds of instruments and amusing pranks that the Orientals used at their feasts now had to entertain the Romans as well. They began to hold luxurious banquets and make the foods more delicate and tasty. The cook, who to the Romans had previously been one of the lowest of the slave rabble, was now held to be of great value.

In a word, things that the Romans had thought appropriate only for servants now began to be regarded as superb and useful arts. We can see from this that our noble instrument and the art of cooking had the same fate, rising in esteem at the same time. We are shown how it looked at the time by an old Roman marble piece, in which we see a few people lying on a couch eating, according to ancient custom, with a number of female servants around. Apart from the crowd there is a chair, upon which a woman is sitting and playing a lute strung with three or four strings. The lute player has been extracted alone from the old marble, because this aspect is not as well known as the banquets of the ancients.

Now this is a beautiful proof that the fingerboard and neck of our instrument were affixed by the Asian peoples, (as can be seen above, very simply made), whereas it previously consisted only of a body. Here it already bears resemblance to a lute, although it was continuously improved after that time, as simplicity always precedes complexity. At this point, all other writers are quite right when they ascribe three strings to our instrument, because it may well have been so after it lost its crossribs and assumed more similarity to our lute of today.

These are the kinds of female lutenists who are called *psaltriae* in the above-cited passage in Livy, and *fidicinae* in Plautus, who describes just such a splendid feast.[v] Plautus introduces into his comedy a messenger who tells of the Babylonian magnificence as he had seen it and of how the most beautiful male and female slaves had been brought to Rome to entertain with such instruments. After that time masters were even kept in Rome, who were required to give lessons to the Roman knights and most distinguished aristocrats. We are told by Alexander that Appius Claudius, who had marched several times to triumph, Gabinus, Marcus Caecilius, and Licinius Crassus danced well and played quite well on various musical instruments. To these distinguished admirers of noble music we can add Decius Syllas and Catonem Censorius.[w] Those who today are called virtuosi were then called *artifices*.

Because Plato expressly desired that first and foremost the nation's youth should be instructed in music, so that they would apply themselves with greater pleasure to other serious studies, the Greeks held musicians in such high esteem that no one could pass for a soothsayer or a wise and clever man unless he understood music. Themistocles was thus thought a clumsy man, because he could not play the lyre, but only desired to play the *testudine*, like Besard.

Pythagoras, one of the most ancient philosophers, recommended noble music to youth merely because they could dampen the violent, sudden rush of fever with it and thereby be deterred from many silly excesses. It is indeed still a valuable medicine today.

Now Svetonius tells us in his life of Emperor Nero that this ruthless tyrant played a musical instrument. Its innocent pleasure, to be sure, could not improve his morals, because ever since his youth his natural instincts had been more inclined to vice than to virtue. He held his instrument in such esteem that he had the laurels he won in the contest hung on the statue of Augustus and worshipped them.[x] It is almost impossible to determine what kind of instrument it was because of the varying designations, since it is sometimes called *cithara* and sometimes *lyra*. I, for my part, lean toward the side that maintain the latter, because on the coins stamped under Nero's reign the instrument resembles Apollo's harp more than Mercury's lute.

Lampridius, in Chapter Thirty-two of his life of the Emperor Heliogabalus, mentions an instrument called *pandura*, with which this inhuman emperor is said to have amused himself, just as Nero did with his *cithar*. Pollux says it was *trichordon*, or strung with three strings. Varro and Isidore maintain that the name of this instrument is a foreign word that had its origin in the Assyrian language, and Pollux, in Book Four, Chapter Nine, names the Assyrians as the inventors of it.

Every reader will still have fresh in his memory what I said about the confusion of authors in naming instruments. I do not think that Varro's and Isidore's opinion is opposed to mine, in that we must consider that Assyria is an Asiatic province, called Cusistan today, and is not so far away from Egypt as other parts of the earth are. In addition, *pandura* is a falsified word and means just that instrument that Scaliger called *lyra testudinea* and the Greeks *cithara*, but the Romans called *testudineus*. Today there is a family of imperfect lutes that are called *pandur*, *pandor*, or even *mandor*, and we will therefore not go wrong if we proceed from the different name to the thing itself, as Salomon von Til does, and determine that Heliogabalus used none other than this instrument for his amusement, particularly if we recall the above-illustrated ancient marble and its Asian origin.

Thus I have endeavored to show how, in my opinion, our instrument came to Italy and what its nature was. In the following chapter, I will strive to explain how, after much confusion in the Occident, it was rediscovered and came to the Franks and subsequently to the Germans.

CHAPTER V

The Rediscovery of Our Instrument, and How it Subsequently Came From the Franks to the Germans

JUST as all arts and sciences rise in esteem when they find the enthusiasts and admirers they deserve, they decline when these are absent, and when Mars swings his terrible, murderous sword against lands and peoples, and against innocence itself. The Roman Empire, which had previously expanded its boundaries from time to time, discovered in the third century after the birth of Christ that its greatness was not secure against barbarian attacks and the violence of many wild peoples, so that one could finally say:

> Where the shining weapons ring
> Can, alas, no muses sing.

In such times scholarship, as well as the other arts, was in a very bad state. What had previously been in flower had to be sought out anew, as it were, from the dust and ashes, rot and decay, and from the ruins of many destroyed cities and palaces. The magnificent and most praiseworthy Anicius Manlius Torquatus Severinus Boethius was the one who was driven by the charm of scholarship and other arts and sciences to rebuild the dilapidated and destroyed empire of the muses and defend it against the tyranny of dark and gloomy oblivion. He lived in the sixth century, was Roman mayor, and was unfortunate enough to be arrested in the year 524 by the Ostrogothic King Theodoric because of the jealousy of a secret understanding with the Emperor Justinian, or, as some think, because Boethius wanted to restore the old Roman Republic, and was beheaded together with his father-in-law Symachus. Although it is most regrettable that such a light of the world should be extinguished in such a cruel and unnatural manner, the rays of honor and truth still glow nonetheless under his ashes. Bertius, who took the praiseworthy effort to immortalize this great man through his writings, eulogizes him, maintaining that he had no equal among the Greek and Latin writers,[y] and that he was the most subtle logician, the most exemplary theologian, the most industrious and unflagging mathematician, the most artful mechanician, the most pleasant musician, and most magnificent orator and poet. Gerbertus, former Bishop of Rheims, testifies in a poem written in his honor, that Boethius exceeded the Greeks and reilluminated scholarship.[z]

Martianus Rota says that Boethius would have brought music to its highest peak had he not been hindered by death.[aa] The author of the *Edelmann* (who is thought to be Counsellor Winckler, formerly of Breslau), recalls in his discourse on ancient and modern music a Boethius who was supposed to have invented an instrument that he calls *citarme*. He is in doubt whether or not this instrument is our guitar of today, but he is certainly of the opinion that the guitar led to the lute, and the lute to the chitarrone or theorbo. The learned Society of Trevoux considers the six-course lutes to be the oldest,[ab] although Praetorius goes further and ascribes four courses of double strings to it. Thus there is no doubt that the above-mentioned Boethius was the one who rediscovered our instrument, which already had its appropriate lute form, improved it, and raised it in esteem after its period of slumber.

Because the *citarme* or *citharra* [guitar] even today are a kind of imperfect lute, and those that have from four to six courses are called *panduren* or *mandoren*, and since these types are supposed to have existed in early medieval times, [Winckler's] doubt is finally erased. Previously, this instrument was known in Italy, until King Clodovaeus of the Franks heard about its convenience and asked King Theodoric for someone who could play it. Now because King Theodoric thought very highly of the above-mentioned Boethius, and in the beginning, by virtue of his splendid scholarship, had trusted him well, he wrote to him and asked him to choose a good and skillful master of the lute. He knew that Boethius had, so to speak, mastered or fathomed this arduous discipline or art.[ac]

Thus we can see how our worthy instrument came to the Franks. But now a few more doubts are raised; for instance, the French are loath to let the Germans have the honor of having named them and, as it were, given them their origin. Some French writers say that the so-called Franks, or *Franci,* were originally ancient Gauls who, because of their numbers, crossed the Rhine and later returned to their fatherland, as Herr von Puffendorff observed. Meanwhile, Herr von Irnhoff says that the Bishop of Rheims called Clodovaeus, at his baptism, a *Sicamber*, which was doubtless a German people. Be that as it may, all other credible authors agree that a German colony that called itself *Francos*, or free people, crossed the Rhine and took Gaul. There have also been many who have showed the French the contrary.

Because my work is here to proceed from the chief transformations of entire peoples to the fate of our instrument, I hope I have not gone wrong in arguing the precise old attachments or blood friendship of the two nations and many other things that the Franks inherited from the Romans and the Germans shared. The Carolingians ruled both Germany and France, and Germany did not exist until the division by Louis the Pious, when it was passed to Louis, one of his sons.

CHAPTER VI

The Most Famous Masters of Music Who Lived in Ancient, Medieval, and Modern Times or Who are Still Living, and How They Served Our Instrument

HITHERTO I have been concerned with examining the fate of our instrument and how it moved from one nation to another. Now we shall observe those individuals who have served it. The famous and soundly learned Pater Anastasius Kircher took special pains to examine the instruments of the ancient Hebrews. From an old manuscript he found in the Vatican library, he produces a few instruments, some of which resemble lutes and some of which resemble guitars still common today. I would like to print the illustrations here for the reader's general edification and differentiation.

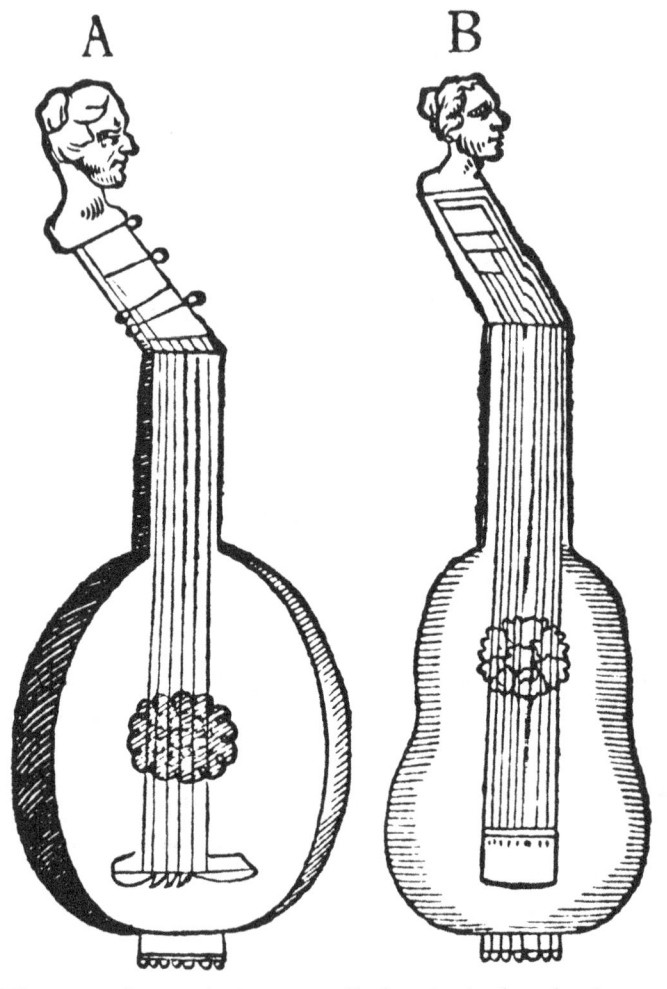

The one denoted *A* was called *minnin* by the learned Rabbi Scilte Sibborim, the other, marked *B*, *machul*. Now I do not wish to consider here how they were played, because opinions differ substantially, but I will merely point out that even the ancient Hebrews had instruments that in exterior form looked almost exactly like our lute. I will also pass over what Asaph, Eman Ezraita, Ethan Ezrachi, and

Asir, Elcana, and Abiasaph, the three sons of Coreh, accomplished and will only mention the singer Idithun and the *citharadus*, which was very well known among the ancient Hebrews. Many consider him to be Orpheus. However, Gregorius Nazianzenus contests this and, in the *Carmine Nicobuli*, considers Orpheus to be not a musician but rather a famous orator. Tomas Burnetius, in *Archiol. Philosoph.*, considers Orpheus a famous philosopher, theologian, and legislator who lived immediately after the time of Moses and taught the wild and barbaric, uncultured people good manners and a religion.

Since Orpheus is far older, and the above-mentioned Idithun lived in the time of Solomon, those who confuse the two have committed a great error. I will also not dwell upon the king and prophet David, because scholars and the ancient church fathers cannot agree on what kind of an instrument he played, although even Franciscus speculates that it was a lute. It will not be necessary to warm over what others have thought of Arion and Linus. But Horace says that Amphion played the lute.[ad] From this it is clear that he [Amphion] was a famous musician and orator; one can read about this Ainphion in Plato's *Laws*, Book III. Horace also tells us how this instrument was strung at the time Amphion played it. He says it was strung with seven strings,[ae] and that Amphion was a student of Mercury.

Sebastian Ochsenkuhn tells us who increased the number of strings on the instrument.[af] He thought this instrument was strung with only seven strings because that was the number of the planets, but if we consider that the ancients made much of the seventh number, even thinking it sacred, this does not seem so ridiculous, according to their principles.[ag]

Cornelius Nepos, who describes the lives of various Greek generals, mentions in his *Vita Epaminondae* some Greek musicians called Dionysius, Damon, and Lamprus. Dionysius was a teacher of Epaminondae, whom he was required to teach to play and sing to the *cithar*, or a kind of lute. All three, incidentally, enjoyed special importance and repute in Greece.[ah] Dionysius was born a Theban, and Plutarch, in his book on music, placed him among the lyric poets, among whom Pindar and Lamprus are especially famous. In Book IV of *The Republic*, Plato lauded Damon very highly; it was even fancied that Damon's music could be changed as little as the commonwealth. Lamprus is also extolled gloriously by Plutarch in Chapter I, and by Athenaeus.

We have already discussed who rediscovered our instrument in Italy and it will not be necessary to repeat it here, for I am determined to speak below about those authors in Italy, France, and Germany who were outstanding in their time and contributed something to the lute. For now, I will only speak of a few other ancient masters.

Cranzius, in Book V, Chapter Three of his *Daniae*, and Olaus Magnus tell of a very strange effect of our instrument, namely that King Eric III of Denmark was driven by its power to such frenzy that he committed many murders. The artist responsible for this is not named, but it is recalled that he actually accomplished everything that he claimed he could. He claimed he wanted to make the cheerful sad, the sad merry, the angry meek, and the meek mad. A king who left behind the reputation of being by nature kind and meek and not inclined to cruelty[ai] had to bequeath his kingdom to his son and depart for the Promised Land, according to the custom of the time, to atone for the sins he had thereby committed, which is very dubious. Kircher ponders the matter intently, first wanting to shove the blame onto the devil, then convincing himself that the unknown artist already knew the effect that the music or his instrument would have upon the king and was forced to play for fear of being poorly thought of if he were disobedient. For my part, I doubt seriously whether art could have risen to the point where it could move the passions there in the cold north, especially with this instrument and at that time, since everything was periodically in a bad state of affairs. However, I do not wish to deny that music can occasionally effect something extraordinary.

I will not mention the men who were bitten by the tarantulas, because this is much too well known and has other causes. However, the Breslau physicians say that the homesickness of the Swiss could be caused by a certain melody. Since I have seen this melody and found that it looks like a cowherd's song, it could well be that their uncommon love for their fatherland and the recollection of their vocation, which is generally cattle-breeding, of which they are reminded by said melody, turns their minds away from merry things and they fall into deep yearning.

Every man has in his nature joy and sadness, but in differing degrees. Such passions become, according to the character of the subjects, more or less active, and it is entirely possible that a person can be harmed as much by excess joy as excess sadness. Each stringed instrument has the power to move air and to drive this air, harmonious in its motion, against the *tympanum* or eardrum by vibrations, so that it is communicated to the nerves and subsequently to the life spirits. But it is a bit difficult to believe that a person could be thereby separated from his rational soul, although a learned Englishman, Robert Douth, or South as he is called by others, mentions in his *Musica incantante* or *poemate* a man who through music was driven to such frenzy that even the artist who was playing his instrument was in danger.

One thing is certain, when someone uses chromaticism on an instrument, the life spirits are necessarily lulled with the slow and rough motion and consequently the circulation of the blood is hampered a bit in its otherwise swift movement, stopped, and brought to serious attention. Where the air is driven faster by the sound, a person feels more liveliness than usual, particularly because in sensuous matters one depends a great deal on external objects. The chief element in this case is the inner disposition of the man who can be driven to madness. Even today we know that people are found who are so stirred by very bad things, that they could expect nothing but death if these things were not removed from their presence. Selimenes was ready to give up the ghost because of the sight of a calf's head, which by nature he could not stand. Tysander fell into a swoon when he saw a cat near him. Philotes began to weep when he saw a periwig being combed out.

The powerful emotions that arise from external objects only affect a few persons, less because of the objects themselves than because of the faults instilled in their souls by their mothers. Since Kircher noted that the removal of Eric's servant would not have been necessary, because music does not work the same wonders with everyone, I came upon the idea that something other than music must be the cause.[aj] For it would necessarily follow that if this stemmed from music and not from natural faults, we would today see such atrocities hourly, since all people have organs for hearing. Moreover, I believe that those who tell such stories lived during times when more fables than truths were heard, and the whole matter is not as serious as has been asserted.

The other master whom we will now consider is the famous David Rizzio. The author of *Conversations in the Realm of the Dead (Gespräche im Reiche der Todten),* as well as many other writers, maintains that he was a lutenist. However, George Buchanan does not mention this in his history of Scotland, but says only that Rizzio was a singer and musician.[ak] He was born in Turin and was instructed in music by his father, because he was not wealthy. After he had learned a proper profession, according to the fashion of the time, he went to the Court of Savoy. However, he did not find what he was looking for until he finally traveled to Scotland with the Savoyan ambassador Moretti, who had to negotiate with the famous Queen Mary. Because Moretti, who was also not particularly wealthy, could not keep him any longer, he tried his luck at the Scottish court and was successful, after a long wait and many tribulations.

The unfortunate Queen Mary, who was later beheaded, was an uncommon lover of music and had a fine orchestra that consisted mostly of Frenchmen. But no one pleased the great queen more than Rizzio; she even made him her secretary. She often secretly had him dine at her table, and even preferred him to her husband Henry, Lord Darnley, who was driven by jealousy to have George Douglas stab Rizzio at the queen's side. It is said that the queen, who was just then pregnant with James VI, was so horrified by the murder that for his whole life the prince could never bear the sight of an unsheathed sword. This queen had such an extraordinary love for David Rizzio that exactly one year to the day after Rizzio died she sacrificed her husband in honor of his spirit and sent him out to exhume Rizzio and bury him royally. This is in brief the career of the fortunate and unfortunate Rizzio, who was believed to play the lute. Because no evidence can be found for it and the circumstances of his life are very admirable, I wanted to communicate to the esteemed reader what reliable sources say about it.

To this point we have been rather uncertain about who has served our noble instrument. But now, after finding better information, the whole matter will become easier, and I will record the following masters in the order that I found them. I wanted to make an effort to take chronological order into account, but it cannot proceed exactly, since from time to time I may err because of lack of sufficient information. Something that is left out here can be brought up later. Because we have left Rizzio in Scotland anyway, I would prefer to remain in the neighborhood and begin with John Dowland, who was very popular in England.

He is called a superb English or angelic lutenist by Besard. Because Dowland knew that a man learns something not only for himself but also for others, he published various books and works on this instrument in about 1619.[5]

[Gregory] Huwet in Juliers, [Jakob] Reys in Gelderland,[a1] Diomedes [Cato] in Sarmatia, and Laurencini in Rome won for themselves great honor and fame with their lutes. In

---

5. John Dowland's last publication, a reprint of his *The first Booke of Songs or Ayres*, appeared in 1613. For a complete list of his works, see Diana Poulton, *John Dowland, His Life and Works* (London, 1972), pp. 516–520.

Paris a man called Camillus was famous. He may doubtless have been one of the earliest lutenists in France. In Meissen the Drusinas excelled in their time. All these famous masters are mentioned by M. Christoph Hunichius in a eulogy he composed for [Johannes] Rude, who will be further discussed below. I will include it here because of its cleverness.[am]

One thing is certain, our splendid instrument was already much in use by 1415,[6] or even earlier, because the world-famous lute maker Lucas Maler lived at this time. We do not actually know, however, what sort of famous masters there were in those days. After that time, Hans Newsidler distinguished himself with published works.[7] He lived in Nuremberg in 1547 and was quite successful in improving the lute, which was previously in a state of great imperfection. Therefore we cannot wonder, when looking at the arrangement of the lute fingerboard, how it came to pass that the instrument earned itself a reputation of being difficult. The lute fingerboard, which is indicated with N.1., had so many individual letters that the player had to learn a separate sign for each note. The characters denoted with N.2. are the bass strings and their variant letters as they had to be laboriously picked out in old German tablature. To impress the reader with all the inconvenience of it, I have printed a few beats of their old German tablature as

---

6. According to Ernst Pohlmann *(Laute Theorbe Chitarrone*, 2nd. ed., Bremen, 1972, p. 342), this early date is the result of a forged label in an instrument in Breslau. Maler was active in 1523, as shown by a reference to him in a letter from Frederick of Mantua to Don Hercules of Gonzaga in 1523 (see Lütgendorff, *Die Geigen- und Lautenmacher vom Mittelalter bis zur Gegenwart*, 3rd. ed., vol. II, p. 313).
7. Newsidler's publications appeared between 1536 and 1549 in Nuremberg. See Pohlmann, op. cit., p. 99f.

52

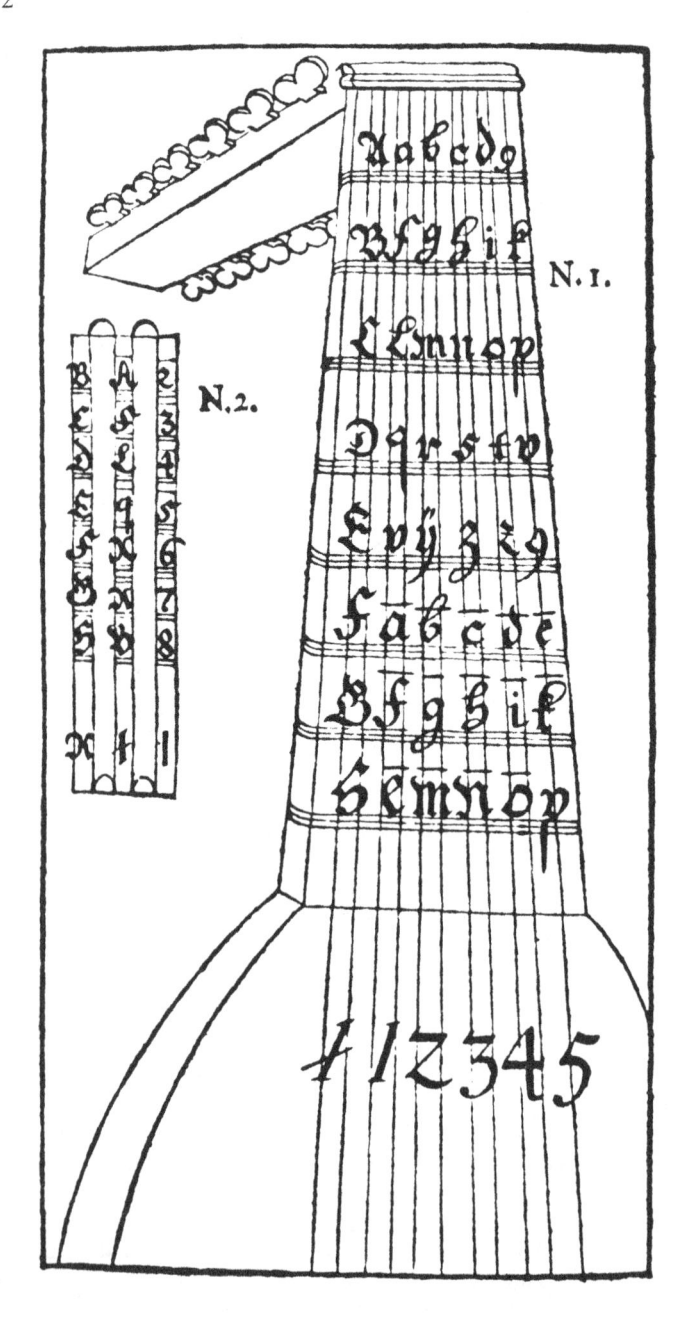

a curiosity, although it serves no purpose other than to be looked at.

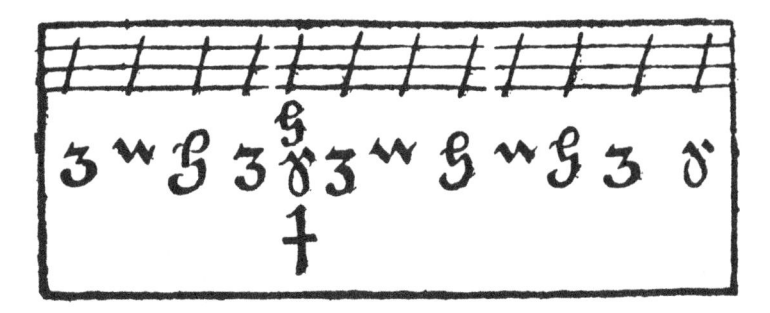

The vertical lines that stand over the tablature letters and are horizontally crossed indicated the beat or the mensuration.

After Hans Newsidler there was another with the same name, and perhaps of the same family, who was famous as a lutenist. He lived in 1574 in Augsburg and was the first to increase the number of strings by one course.[8] For in Sebastian Ochsenkuhn's opinion the lute at first had nine strings according to the Muses, then with Apollo ten, and finally eleven according to the number of the heavenly spheres (laughing, tender friends). Thus [Melchior] Newsidler increased them by one course, and since the tuning in its earliest childhood was **c f a d'**, and afterwards, when the chanterelle and another bass had been added, it was tuned **G c f a d' g'**, the [Melchior] Newsidler stringing was **F G c f a d' g'**, starting with the bass.

He complains a great deal about the previous lack of strings, that much had been left out and the lutenist was

---

8. The seven-course lute with thirteen or fourteen strings was mentioned as early as 1511 by Sebastian Virdung *(Musica getutscht)*, although music was not commonly written for it until much later.

required to invent peculiar, contrived melodies. He writes that these conditions had moved him to consider an improvement.[an] He used odd words to express the pertinent technical terms. For instance, the six (or, as the lute then had, seven) courses he called *Gamaut,* and the basses *Brummer* or *Bomhart,* and the thinner bass strings *Bomhärtlein.* Now the designation *Gamaut* may well have originated in the gamut of Guido of Arezzo, because the musical scale he invented was similarly applied to the lute. The word *Bomhart* seems to resemble the designation of an old deep bass instrument called *Bombard.*

We can assume no more of the younger Newsidler than his good will. As the proverb says: *Ut desint vires tamen est laudanda voluntas.*[9] His intent was good, and we can say: *Et voluisse sat est.*[10] He published several works, including two lute books in Italian tablature (since staff lines had already been invented in 1028, or at the beginning of the eleventh century), to deny the evil rumor that Germans have a crude and simple way of making music. However, when he learned that his good intention of disproving this to foreigners had been misinterpreted as using Italian tablature out of contempt for his fatherland, he desired to regain the good will of his countrymen and to rid himself of the false rumor, so he published for the Germans another book in folio form in German tablature. He also well understood Italian [sic: French] tablature; thus I have inserted a bit of it, as it was fashionable in those days.

---

9. Though physical strength be absent, still one's will is to be praised.
10. Even to have intended it is enough.

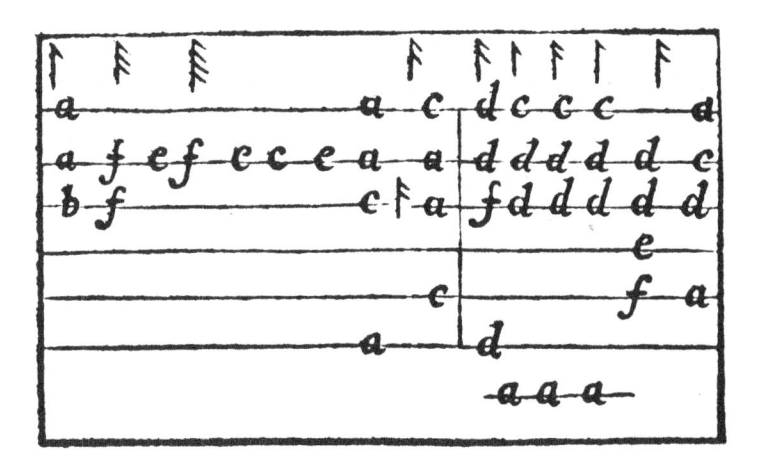

This was the beginning of today's tablature, except that today the signs for indicating the mensuration are completely different. At the time when the two Newsidlers and, after them, still other old masters lived, they first used these signs: ⌈, ⌈, ⌈, ⌈. But later they were changed somewhat and took the following forms:] signified O; ⌐ meant Q, β was then ♩, β had in the measure the time of ♪, and β of ♪. ⌐β meant ♩♩ and ββ meant ♩♪, and ββ was]β.

Here we can imagine what sort of torture it was in those days to accomplish anything on the instrument, because watching both the fingering and mensuration signs made life grim for the player. His pieces consisted of motets, Italian and French pieces, fantasias, dances, passamezzi, and so forth.

Nothing more is known of Hans Vogel than that he was the teacher of the old and very famous Sebastian Ochsenkuhn. It has already been mentioned above where Ochsenkuhn was in service. He published his book on July 26, 1558, at the command of the Elector of the Palatinate, Otto

Heinrich, and it is just as full of fine things as Newsidler's books. On all of the pieces that he published he always put his motto, *"Habe GOtt vor Augen"* (Keep God before your eyes), perhaps in order to admonish each who used them to use them truly out of special fear of God. It would be good if today's musicians always cherished respectable thoughts about their art; many a one would have more money and honor, since this often does not happen.

In the manner of the busy bees, Ochsenkuhn gathered together from all cultivated parts of Europe everything that served his purpose. Thus he equally admired Italians, Frenchmen, and Germans, among whom were Josquin des Prez, Claudianus Benedictus, Johannes Mouton (doubtless a relative of the famous lutenist of this name in France), Gregorius Peschin, Johannes Kilian, Lupus Hellinch, Antonius Fevin, Gombert, Adrian Caen, Jobst von Brandt, Verdelot, and Ludwig Senfl, who composed mostly motets. Ochsenkuhn also set German, Italian, and French pieces by the following masters: Paul Hofhaimer, Caspar Glanner, Steffan Zirler, Wilhelm Breitengraser, Caspar Othmayr, Heinrich Isaac, Martin Zilte, an organist, Stephen Mahu, Thomas Stoltzer, Arcadelt, and Crequillon. All the masters mentioned here contributed much to the culture of our instrument through their compositions, beautiful in their time, for they gave the lutenists something to work on, so that the former had to strive ever harder to impart something from the keyboard to the lute. The melodies were still simple and more full-voiced than *cantabile*, but meanwhile we must not scorn these pieces, because simplicity must always precede perfection.

Hans Gerle was also very famous with regard to the

lute in Nuremberg in 1523. However, further details about him are unknown to me, because to my knowledge he published nothing.[11]

Johannes Albinus lived in Magdeburg in 1596 and exerted great effort and industry to contribute to the improvement of our noble instrument. I have seen a book by him that was very curious and peculiar, for I was astonished at the many characters he invented to properly explain the instrument theoretically.[12] He played German tablature as well as number tablature, and instead of making the instrument easier, he created more confusion, darkness, and disorder with the multitude of rules, numbers, letters and other characters. Meanwhile, I believe he would have helped and contributed more to the instrument had he been able to teach clearly and briefly what was pertinent to his instrument. It was the fashion in those days to use the darkest and silliest terminology for true art and wisdom. This master had the same fate as the scholastics, metaphysicians, and alchemists who were uncommonly loved and admired, not for the content of their works, but for the terrible sounding words.

Melchior Schmidt lived in Nuremberg. He was born in 1608, but when he died is uncertain. He was a man of good resolution and was very famous with regard to the lute. He was, I believe, the first to discard the old German tablature, together with all other confusion, and adopt the Italian tablature, which was very popular for its brevity and

---

11. Gerle published several books of tablature and instructions. See Jane Pierce, "Hans Gerle: Sixteenth-century Lutenist and Pedagogue," *Journal of the Lute Society of America*, Vol. VI (1973), pp. 17–29.

12. Baron's reference to this book is the only evidence of its existence. No known copy has survived.

clarity. Once, while he was playing in the presence of many distinguished aristocrats, something strange happened that would have caused confusion in another person. He did not allow himself to be troubled, but remained unmoved with the greatest *presence d'esprit*. He applied himself vigorously to the theorbo, and he can be seen, occupied with his music, very artfully painted on a wing of the organ at St. Sebald [in Nuremberg?].

Johann Welter was in service as a musician at the Nuremberg Chapel. He was born in 1614, and died in 1666. We cannot know exactly the extent of his merits in art for serving the lute, since his pieces have mostly been lost because of the carelessness of those who did not understand them. Yet it is certain that in his time he was one of the most distinguished of those who were concerned with the cultivation of our noble instrument.

Now after each of the above-mentioned masters had done his part and left behind much for posterity to ponder, Herr Johann Rude or Rudenius took this into consideration. In the month of August, 1600, on the encouragement of the Most Serene Lords, Johann Ernest and August, brothers and Dukes of Braunschweig-Lüneburg, he published in Leipzig a collection by the most famous masters, whose pieces he had set in lute tablature after the Italian fashion. Because these Maecenaces had blessed him with many kindnesses, he dedicated the work to them in gratitude.[ao] Rude highly recommended this innocent, pure pleasure to the educated because he well knew how man's disposition, fatigued and dejected through serious affairs, could be uplifted and brought to proper use of healthy reason, and the life spirits could be again led to harmony through this instrument.[ap] It is common for all arts and sciences to be often misused, but an evil employment of this noble art cannot harm its honor or perfection in the least.[aq] The industry that Rude applied to music, as well as to the study of law, was tireless. Thus he collected all the good material he found, even among foreigners, and applied it to the lute. To accomplish this purpose he could not do better than to arrange pieces by Italians, Frenchmen, and Germans who, even in those days, as far as their insight permitted, admirably served music, and to transcribe them for our instrument.[ar]

Those who contributed much to his design were Giovanni Maria Nanio, Alessandro Striggio, Girolamo Conversi, Luca Marenzio, Girolamo Vespa, Pietro Vinci, Noel Faignient, Giovanni Pietro Manenti, Giovanni Ferretti, Philippe de Monte, Pomponio Nenna, Stefano Felis, Giovanni di Maque, Giovanni Gabrieli, Hippolito Baccusi, Hubert Waelrant, Francesco Rovigo, Leandro Mira, Hippolito Sabino, Giaches de Wert, Andrea Gabrieli, Lelio Bertani, Orazio Vecchi, Teodoro Rizzii (who was perhaps a close relative of the unfortunate Rizzio, who was massacred in Scotland), Jacques Regnart, Hans Leo Hassler, Bernardo Mosto, Ferrabosco, Gasparo Costa, Vincenzo Neri, Gregor Aichinger, Giovanni Francesco Violanti, Giacomo Gastoldi, Cipriano de Rore, Giovanni Pisoni, Annibal Stabile, and Orlando di Lasso. Among the Germans, Leonhard Lechner was a favorite of his.

According to the fashion of the time, the pieces consisted of all kinds of Italian and German songs, fantasias on spiritual hymns, pavans, galliards, padovanas, intradas, and so forth. Because this master had a special drive to raise this noble art, not only the above-mentioned Hunichius but also M. Johann Richter distinguished himself with the composition of a pretty panegyric in his honor. But since I wish to cultivate the utmost brevity here, I must refrain from printing it until another time, for it is a bit long.

The admirable and learned Jean Baptiste Besard of Besançon in Burgundy reaped great honor with his *Isagoge in artem testudinarium,* which he published in Augsburg in 1617, and in which he began to proceed scientifically with this subject, as far as its state of cultivation permitted. He was a Doctor of Laws and a profound musician as well. As a learned man, he found it easier than others to observe this discipline with the appropriate order. The masters of whom he made use were Laurencini of Rome, Diomedes Cato, Fabritio Dentice of Naples, Alfonso Ferrabosco, Hortensius Perla of Padua, Pomponius of Bologna, Charles Bocquet, Jean Perichon, Johannes Edinthonius, de Vaumeny, Ballard of Paris, Mercure, Victor de Montbuysson of Avignon, Cydriac Rael of Bourges, Jakob Reys, Elias Mertel, Valentin Greff-Bakfark of Hungary, Adalbert Dlugorai of Poland, and John Dowland of England. The last of these thought so highly of his work that he could do no better than to republish what Besard wrote on the study of *modum* or order on the lute.[13] Besard also wrote *Novus partus sive concertationes musicae,* which consists more of a relation of various harmonies than, melodic passages and *cantabile.*

I was curious and tuned the lute in the old manner of that time, and I cannot sufficiently describe the remarkable effect his compositions had. For I heard tones that blended

---

13. Some instructions by Besard (from an appendix to the *Thesaurus Harmonicus)* are given in English translation in Robert Dowland, *Varietie of Lute Lessons* (London, 1610), pp. 5–12.

together well but, to tell the truth, there was little or no melody. Be that as it may, they nevertheless wrote concerti with three and four lutes in this manner and marveled at the wonders they possessed.

This Besard no longer used the old, above-mentioned signs to denote the mensuration, but rather already set notes, as is customary today, above the tablature and had his lute strung with up to ten courses. The German translation of his instructions is dedicated to certain old, noble families, the Zobels and Puroners. His *Novus partus*, however, is dedicated to Ernest, Duke of Holstein, Schauenburg, and Sternberg, and various clever minds wrote the following figure of him:

"Caesari erat liber iste tuus Besarde dicandus
Dignus at his Comes est Caesaris esse comes."

"Intacta e cerebro est Pallas Iovis orta: Besardi
Prodit ab ingenio partus hic ecce bono."[14]

This man, because of his erudition and skill in music, enjoyed such great stature that many learned people eagerly endeavored to immortalize his merits with all sorts of pretty and ingenious tributes. C.C.N.a.B. in Augsburg, Mart. Anth. Balletzius from Holland, Christophorus Forleger from Nuremberg, all from noble families, honored him with fine panegyrics, quite apart from what M. Petrus Meyderlin, M. Moses Hermann, Johannes Hontemius, and an unknown P.H.c.d.A. wrote in his honor. Among others the following epigrams are noteworthy, since by shifting the letters from

---

14. "This book of yours, Besard, ought to be told of to Caesar; This 'companion' is worthy of being a companion of Caesar." "Virgin Pallas was born from the head of Zeus; This creation comes forth from the good talent of Besard."

the words "Johannes Baptista Besardus Vesontinus" we can derive *da bona, Sirenes ut tu Bonus anteis ipsas item: Bonus. Pieridas anteis; tantus est.*[15] The following French verses are also admirable for their thought:

> Ce viez Orphée dont tout le monde parle
> Brave enchantoit les rochers et les Bois
> Mais celui ci d'une science egale
> Peut bien charmer les Princes et le Rois.[16]

We must honor him because he contributed what the knowledge of the time demanded.

Now we shall turn to those who had already begun to unite harmonious essence with *cantabile* and who knew how to choose unconstrained and pretty melodies. The two Reusners, father and son, who were Silesians by birth, were doubtless the first to endeavor to compose unconstrained melodies that agree with the spirit of the instrument, since in the old days they had to make do mostly with transcribed pieces. The father, Esaias Reusner, published his *Lauten-Lust* in Breslau in 1668;[17] it consisted of preludes, padovanas, courantes, sarabandes, gigues, gavottes, and other pieces. His son, however, who was more *galant* in

---

15. Bestow your wealth, so that you, excellent man, will thereby surpass the Sirens themselves. You will excel the Muses; so great a man is he.
16. Ancient Orpheus, of whom everyone speaks,
Gallantly enchanted the rocks and trees.
But this man, with equal skill,
Can well charm princes and kings.
17. Esaias Reusner the Elder (date of birth unknown, died between 1660 and 1680) published his *Musikalischer Lust-Garteri* in Breslau in 1645. His son Esaias the Younger (1636–1679) published *Delitiae Testudiriis* in 1667, and reprinted it in 1668 as *Delitiae Testudiriis. Oder Erfreuliche Lauteri-Lust.* The *Neue Lauteri-Fruchte* appeared in Berlin in 1676. For a list of his other publications see Pohlmann, p. 112f.

composition than his father, distinguished himself considerably in those days when he published his *Lauten-Früchte*. His sacred songs and hymns are set very well, so that one can still use them today for private enjoyment. He strove to practice *cantabile* on the instrument and to bring a better, pure harmonious essence into his pieces.

Jakob Büttner came even closer to the goal in 1683 when he published one hundred and seven "extremely charming and beautiful" (to use his words) lute pieces in Nuremberg, according to the latest and most *galant* method of playing the lute at that time.[18]

The Bohemian Count Losy, very famous for his extraordinary dexterity and gifted with a great mind, brought our noble instrument to such high stature, with respect to both its esteem and its cultivation, that we are justified in naming it today the queen of all musical instruments, as Besard does.[as] It was rightly looked upon by Praetorius as an ornamenting instrument, with which one can decorate, embellish, and spice other music. Now we can exclaim quite suitably with Horace:

"*Vec loquax olim neo grata nuncet
divitum mensis et amica templis.*"

                        item, Ode XXXII.

"*Grata Testudo Jovis o laborum
dulce lenimen, mihicunque salverite vocanti.*"[19]

Count Losy is said to have been so pensive about the

---

18. This date is a typographical error. The *Pieces de luth...* of Jacques Bittner, presumably the same lutenist, appeared in 1682 with no place of publication indicated.
19. "Welcome to the feasts of Jove, o sweet and healing balm of troubles, help me whenever I call upon you in proper fashion."

instrument that he often took it along on journeys, and when a good idea came to him, he had the horses stopped and recorded it in his tablet. It is said that the Most Exalted and Glorious Emperor Leopold, who was a great Maecenas and protector of scholars and artists, made Losy a count because of his skill on the lute.[20] It was nothing unusual for His Most Highly Esteemed Imperial Majesty to knight a true virtuoso of rare genius and good manners. This famous master so successfully combined the new Italian and French method of playing the lute that he not only composed very charmingly *cantabile* for the ear, but also artfully and profoundly. His praiseworthy life lasted approximately eighty years, and in 1721 he exchanged temporality for eternity. The following was written of his death in Prague:

> It is now three weeks ago that our beloved father of the lute, namely Count Losy, left everything behind and journeyed from this world into eternity. When it was announced to him ,three weeks ago that he would not recover, he said, "*Á Dio* lutes, *á Dio* violins!" The lutes and violins were then turned upside down and black bands were tied upon them to proclaim that the lute was also dead, and so all lutes should mourn for him.

Achatius Casimir Huelse was once the valet of the highly esteemed Count Losy, and later lived in Nuremberg. Because Losy had profited well by him, the Count held him in such

---

20. Jan Antonín (Johann Anton) Losy, Count von Losynthal, was born in 1650 and died in 1721. His father was ennobled in 1647, made a baron in 1648 and a count in 1655 for his part in the defense of Prague against the Swedes during the Thirty Years War. Thus the lutenist was born a nobleman, and was also one of the richest men in Bohemia. See Emil Vogl, "Zur Biographie Losys (1650–1721)," *Die Musikforschung*, Vol. XIV (1961), pp. 189–192.

esteem that whenever he traveled through Nuremberg he sent for Huelse and gave him gifts. Huelse was a man full of jolly and ingenious ideas, who could imitate anyone's voice and speech so naturally that listeners were astonished. He was also a composer himself, and he derived his greatest pleasure from expressing all sorts of affections in his composition. He was so successful at this that he exceeded all Frenchmen, for the French commonly give grand names to their pieces, but they have as little to do with the music as heaven does with the earth. In middle age, Huelse had the misfortune to suffer a stroke that left him so disfigured that although he lived quite a long time afterwards, he resembled a monster more than a man.

[Philipp] Wieland composed many *Overturen*. Riwitzky is considered by some to be a Polish nobleman. He is notable for his accomplished technique, and served as court lutenist to the present King of Poland. He died about fifteen or sixteen years ago. Schlinsky was a Bohemian by birth, and he composed rather difficult but quite melodious pieces. [Wolff Jakob] Lauffensteiner and Schaffnitz both served the Electorate of Bavaria, the former as valet, the latter as lieutenant. Each composed many fine things. [Ferdinand Ignaz] Hinterleithner and [Johann Georg] Weichenberger are Viennese and have also given many pieces to the world under their names. The latter particularly is said to be popular for his skill. Haussler was born in Prague but lived mostly in Breslau. He was rather accomplished, despite the fact that in Poland the index finger of his left hand was lamed by a blow in a fight, so that he could not use it for anything but barring. In his time, his pieces were very popular.

Antonius Eckstein and Aurius, or, as others have it,

Audius Dix, both of whom lived in Prague, paid their debt to nature in 1721.[21] We find in their pieces good melody, full-voiced texture, and *cantabile*. Herr [Andreas Bohr] von Bohrenfels is the Imperial Court Lutenist, but because he is very guarded with his pieces, he is not known outside Viennese society. Meley, who applied himself to the study of law in Leipzig as well as to music and afterwards graduated as a licentiate, is very famous for many compositions and for his *solidité*. The noble Count [Johann Adam von] Questenberg, who still lives in Vienna, also distinguished himself admirably on this pleasant instrument. There is in his compositions an extraordinary spirit and expression.

Now after I have had the honor of reporting the meritorious service to the lute of many distinguished men and other fine people, I must relate what the famous and beloved Weiss family from Silesia has accomplished. The father of the children, who are all still living, was a profound musician, lutenist, and theorbist. The two sons, Herr Sylvius Leopold and Herr Sigismund Weiss, together with their sister, who is now married to a pastor in the Palatinate, have brought the instrument to the highest peak of perfection. Among these siblings, the elder Herr Sylvius Leopold has especially excelled with his perfect compositions, but his brother is also very fine and is, in addition, an excellent gambist, violinist, and composer. Their lute concerti, trios, and *Galanterie* partitas are so filled with such ingenious, charming, well-connected ideas that one beautiful and exceptional thought accompanies another, as it were.

---

21. Dix's dates are ca. 1669–1719; Eckstein lived ca. 1657–1720. See Emil Vogl, "Aureus Dix und Antoni Eckstein," *Die Musikforschung*, Vol. XVII (1964), pp. 41-45.

Because I have seen several pieces by the elder Herr Weiss and have heard him play, I will take the liberty of saying somewhat more about him. He is the first to show that more could be done on the lute than was hitherto thought possible. And in regard to his skill, I can sincerely testify that it makes no difference whether one hears an ingenious organist performing his fantasias and fugues on a harpsichord or hears Monsieur Weiss playing. In arpeggios he has an extra ordinary full-voiced texture, in expression of emotions he is incomparable, he has a stupendous technique and an unheard-of delicacy and *cantabile* charm. He is a great improviser, for he can play extemporaneously the most beautiful themes, or even violin concerti directly from their notation, and he plays thorough bass extraordinarily well on either lute or theorbo.

About 1708 he went with Prince Alexander Sobiesky to Italy, where he spent a long time in Rome and astonished all the Italians. After the prince went the way of all flesh, Monsieur Weiss returned to Breslau and later entered the royal Polish service; he is presently in Dresden. He also has had the special honor of performing to unusual applause for both living and ruling Imperial Majesties.

For my part, I should wish nothing more than to see this worthy family, a jewel and adornment of our German fatherland, have the same fortune as the world-famous Florentine musician Antonius Squarcialupi, whose likeness the city council in Florence had carved into marble and set before the cathedral doors, so that many would be encouraged by the memorial to their virtue. Yet I believe that if this were to happen, most people would react like Julius Caesar, who began to weep when he saw in Gades the picture of Alexander the Great enthroned, because the latter had accomplished great deeds already in his youth, and Caesar, at his age, had still accomplished nothing special that could contribute to his fame. The most remarkable thing about them is that these noble Weiss siblings had already accomplished great things in their tender youth, and the treasure of art that they began to assemble must have increased markedly in the meantime.

In his *Critica Musica* (Part II, page 152), Herr Mattheson mentioned a strange misfortune of the elder Herr Weiss, namely that in 1722 a violinist almost bit off the last joint of his thumb. This violinist was named Petit and was previously in the service of the Ducal Saxon court at Eisenach, but after he left there he came to Dresden either to be of service or to perform at the royal court. However, because this person neglected one thing or another from the beginning, he accomplished neither goal. Monsieur Weiss, who because of his inborn generosity treated Petit, as a foreigner, with all civility and courtesy, discovered to his surprise that Petit considered him to be the one who had stood in his way. In all probability this presumption was entirely unfounded. Some say he was born in Geneva, Switzerland, others consider him a Frenchman. Be that as it may, he acted in this instance in such a manner that in the future everyone will think of him as either a very jealous person or as someone seeking vengeance at the wrong time. He is said to be in Holland now.

Because the Weissian manner of playing the lute is considered the best, most sound, *galant,* and perfect of all, many have striven to attain this new method, just as the Argonauts sought the Golden Fleece. Monsieur Meusel, by birth a Silesian from Breslau, was one of the first to apply himself to it. This *galant* master has often performed his pleasant lute compositions. When he left Breslau, he first studied at Leipzig, applying himself, aside from music, for several years to the study of law. Afterwards he was called to the court at Zeitz, but when the court was dissolved, he went to Franconia, and then spent some time in Nuremberg with Her Grace the Countess von Bollheim. He then came to the Sovereign Saxon-Gotha court, where he has the good fortune to serve one of the most perfect of sovereigns, and he is still there to this date. His playing consists of alternation between forcefulness and delicacy, as the music demands, and his concerti as well as his suites charm the ear extraordinarily. He is also a fine accompanist.

Herr Johann Michael Kühnel the Elder is a fine gambist and lutenist as well, and his pieces, with which he has made himself known in the *galant* world, are to be highly recommended. The later pieces are far more solid than the early ones, because with time he became much more adept at composition. He composed not only many suites, but also concerti with the lute and viola da gamba and with other appropriate instruments. At first he was in service at the royal Prussian court; from there he came to the ducal Saxon court in Weimar, then to His Excellency, Field Marshall Flemming, and was later in Hamburg.

Monsieur Jacobi from Meissen has also shown all lovers of this beautiful instrument that he is very skilled at composing for the lute. His pieces, although they are somewhat pensive, sound good to the ear, and there is a pleasant spirit in them.

Herr Johann Laurentius Gleim, born in Quedlinburg, also accomplished beautiful things on this instrument. His pieces are speculative but quite charming, and he knows how to alternate cleverly with the middle voices. He also studied law, among other diversions, and spent most of his time in Halle in Saxony.

Monsieur Grave, born not far from Halle, has heard Monsieur Weiss himself and has adopted his method as far as possible. In 1718 he went on tour to Silesia, and after he returned he was engaged at the noble Saxon court in Merseburg, where he died about 1724 of consumption. This fine master studied law in addition to his music. His pieces are harmonious, charming, and *cantabile,* and he played more cleanly than rapidly.

Monsieur [Paul] Gleitsmann, born in Arnstadt in Thuringia, also studied law as well as music in 1716 or 1717 in Leipzig. He eventually went to Prague and profited well there. He is now in the service of the Bishop of Würzburg. His pieces, to which he has applied much industry, are very pleasing.

All the masters mentioned here have earned special merit on this instrument. I wish to be fair and to recall them with all due respect; thus, if someone has been omitted, he can be remembered at another opportunity. For now we shall leave Germany and turn to *galant* France. Monsieur Perault and Pater Bonhour (as the learned Professor Stolle remarks in his *Anleitung zur Historie der Gelahrtheit*) credit the French with everything and the Germans with very little. Whether this is so, and whether they decreed it in truth or out of self-love, I will allow others to judge. An unnamed author, who claims to be Swiss and who deals frequently with both the English and the French, has characterized their virtues and faults perfectly. He says that the French cling close to incidentals and quite often neglect what is real and solid.[at] My business here will be nothing more than to examine how far their *bel esprit* extends in music and on the lute, and leave other matters untouched for now. They boast a great deal about their one and only Lully, although he was not French at all, but Italian. Nonetheless, Monsieur Perault did his best to naturalize him in his book on the lives of the most famous Frenchmen, and Boileau mentions him often with great praise in his poems. The instruments that they extolled were primarily the viola da gamba, transverse flute, and the oboe.

The two Marais, father and son, and Forqueray are very famous as gambists, and their compositions are in some places well known. Yet I believe that Monsieur Hesse, in service at Darmstadt in Hessen, does not have to yield an inch to any of the three, as highly as they are praised, for it is said that he has learned all that the French masters have to teach.

On the oboe, des Noyers, who was formerly in the service of Prince von Vaudemont, is said to have been excellent. Herr Nemeitz, who was the distinguished Court Councillor at Waldeck, declared after his sojourn in Paris that in his whole life he had never heard the like. However, I do not know whether the Councillor ever heard the world-famous Peter Klesch in Berlin, and if this should happen, perhaps the Councillor's enthusiasm could be lessened. The transverse flute is very popular with the French, although this instrument had its origin in Germany and is thus called *allemande*.

In regard to the lute, the French have not accomplished much in particular. Their most famous masters are [Denis?] Gaultier, who is considered to be one of the earliest, although he wrote his pieces for our present-day lute.

[Charles] Mouton and Dufaut followed their own genius and neglected the *cantabile* element. [Jacques] Gallot gave his pieces such strange names that one must ponder hard how they connect with the music, particularly when he tried to express thunder and lightening on the lute. It is too bad that he did not indicate when it lit and struck. A certain author, of whom we can more readily approve, composed the siege of Vienna on the lute and indicated above the passages: "Here the cannons thunder, here the wounded Turks howl, here they are driven to flight."

One seldom finds a French piece that does not have the name of a *galant* lady after whom, if it pleased her, the piece was named—for instance, *La des premont, La marquise, La solitaire, La belle magnifique, La desolée, La pleureuse,* and so forth. This is not to mention others that they named after their patrons and good friends. I cannot imagine why, except that they want to imitate the poets who wrote verses in honor of their beautiful mistresses, in order to similarly immortalize them, as Ovid and especially Petrarch did with his Laura. The name should always fit the music, and where the third person comparative is dragged in by the hair seems to me to be charlatanry and affectation, as though the composer wanted to entertain with the name more than the music.

[Jacques de] Saint-Luc is one of the best, for he always allows something lyrical to flow into his pieces, and he is praised by Herr von Besser in the description of the nuptials of the Most Serene Crown Prince Frederick of Kassel with Princess Louise Dorothee Sophie of the Electorate of Brandenburg, which took place in 1700.[au]

With regard to the characteristics of the French, they

too often change voices, so that one cannot even recognize the melody, and, as already mentioned, there is little *cantabile* to be found, particularly because they regard it as very fashionable to brush back chords on the lute with the right hand, just as on the guitar; a constant hopping around is required to give spirit and life to the pieces. I have also observed that they consider it delicate to use the deep basses very little, preferring instead the middle range. This is to say nothing of the simple melodies I often hear. But one does find a few pieces that are rather well composed. In this respect Herr Mattheson is absolutely right when he satirizes the scratching away at allemandes in the Parisian style. However, whether his entire judgment of the lute is conceived according to philosophy and art will be shown below at length.

CHAPTER VII

The Famous Lute Makers, Their Work, and the True Quality and Virtue of a Lute

Now we have speculated about the history and origin of this noble instrument, together with its famous masters, who began to polish it and further devoted all possible efforts so that it might be even more exalted. I think, then, that it would not be inappropriate to mention something about the famous lute makers, especially since these persons are connected, and lutenist and lute maker cannot exist without each other. Here it will not be necessary to go back much into antiquity and torment ourselves with many uncertain opinions, but rather it will be best to remain with probability and irrefutable truth.

In the fifth chapter we already considered Boethius, the Roman mayor who lived in the sixth century after the birth of Christ, and the fact that he, in addition to other fine sciences and great scholarship, also had great knowledge in mechanics and mathematics. We know that he was a splendid musician and mechanician, and these sciences are very useful in the invention of instruments. We have also heard that he played the lute and he is considered the restorer of all good arts and sciences. Thus it is probable that when he found traces of it, he reconstructed the lute.

Be that as it may, the learned Society of Trevoux considers

even to this date that the best instruments of this kind are made in Italy and holds that the wood from which instruments in Bologna were made contributed something special to the sound. Now certainly, sweet-sounding Bolognese lutes are found, but is the wood the sole cause of the sweet sound (*Wohl-Klang*)? This is a topic that would be worth further investigation. It is true that the drier the wood, the better it is for instruments. And it makes a great difference whether the tree stood in a good situation while growing and was felled in the right season. Some consider that winter is the best because the wood, being colder, is also necessarily drier, and it is more than well known that the sap has then descended to the roots, which has a positive effect on the sound.

Although all this may well be true, it is nonetheless merely incidental for a good sound, for the essence depends entirely on the luthier. He knows the appropriate mathematical proportions, so that the cavities, height, depth, length and width fit together uniformly. This uniformity (*egalite*) is the reason that an instrument, whether it be of Italian, German, or French wood, sounds good. Thus the lutes that are too deep in the lower part of the body, like a sack, as it were, and have small rosettes or resonance holes are worth little or nothing. But when the lutes are made shallow and have large rosettes, the tone is stout and strong and projects well into the distance. To make a lute with a strong tone the luthier will do well to make somewhat thin bars under the soundboard. This causes the sound, which is caught in the body by the soundhole or rosette (especially when the instrument is oval and flat) to reverberate in a more rapid and light way. If the bars are too wide and numerous, then it will necessarily follow that the tone will linger in the many cavities, and because it is precipitated inwards, as it were, and ever slower in the air before it is driven to the ear, it loses its power.

Here we can see that more is demanded than the quality of wood, as the Society of Trevoux would have us believe.[av] Yet one must proceed cautiously and refrain from putting on too few bars, lest the top soon go to pieces. Then the player, while playing, especially if he is doing so forcefully, would suffer the inconvenience of having the top fly into his face, complete with bars and all the strings.

Good lutes and theorboes are now being made in France as well, and they are occasionally extraordinarily costly. The learned Society of Trevoux assures us that it has heard from a reliable author that a lute made of pure gold had been seen in Paris, worth 32,000 *Reichs-Thaler*.[aw] It does not say who had the lute. I suspect that the aristocrat or master, whoever he is, was more *galant* than artistic, because such an instrument is more to be looked at than really used. I once saw at Herr Hoffman's in Leipzig an old lute of solid copper, heavily gilded on the back with many figures etched upon it, and the top was of black ebony. But when I examined the tone, I found that this instrument sounded more like an old pot than a true lute. Whoever wishes to have a good-sounding instrument will choose good and appropriate wood; therefore, we do not wish to pass over those master luthiers who have made a good name for themselves.

Laux Maler

Lucas Maler is without doubt one of the oldest and best masters who ever made such instruments. He lived about 1415[22] and, we believe, in Bologna, together with Hans Frey. It is remarkable that they already were working in today's fashion, with the bodies oblong, flat, and wide-ribbed. These lutes are esteemed above all others, insofar as there is no fraud and they are original (or, as the technical term has it, *oriental*). They command very high prices, because they are rare and have a magnificent tone. However, we might wish that the artists who can make fine instruments would receive their just rewards during their lifetime, which would benefit them and their families, because such things only amount to useless honors after their death.

Some of the lutes from Füssen are made much too much in the oldest fashion, namely round like an apple, and they are not worth much. However, Raphael Mest, who apprenticed with the famous Michael Hartung in Padua and lived in 1650 and 1627, was one from Füssen who distinguished himself better than others.

Clayss von Pommersbach in Collen, as he signed himself, is also one of the best and oldest. His work is splendid, and a person who has one of his instruments may congratulate himself. The above-mentioned Hans Newsidler, who lived in Nuremberg, applied himself not only to music but also to lute-making. I have seen bodies by him with the year

---

22. See note 6.

1553 inside. They were somewhat large, of special foreign wood, and looked rather proportionate. Sebastian Rausgler, who lived in 1594 (but I do not know where), made good lutes with wide ribs.

Magnus and Vendelino Tieffenbrucker and Vendelino Venere showed appropriate proportions in their work, and worked in the newest and most highly esteemed fashion, namely oblong or somewhat shallow. The lutes of the Tieffenbruckers are valued far more than the Füssen lutes and are seldom found for sale. These masters lived mostly in Venice between 1500 and 1600.

Paul Belami lived in Paris and earned immortal fame there with his work. He flourished around the year 1612. Hans Fichtholdt, who made splendid lutes in the Italian style in about 1612, should also not be passed over. I do not know, however, where he was resident. His narrow-ribbed work is valued highly by instrument connoisseurs.

[Mattheus] Buchenberg, or Buckenberg, lived in Rome in 1606. He was German by birth, but worked in the Italian fashion with narrow ribs. Some extant theorboes made by him are the most splendid that can be found—oval-round, of a very proportionate size, and with a very delicate, penetrating, metallic tone. Whoever is fortunate enough to possess something by this special and splendid master can cherish it as a true jewel of an instrument. The top or the belly is commonly ornamented with three rosettes after the Roman fashion, so that they can project the tone well.

Antonio Cortaro lived later in Rome in 1614. Christofilo Rochi and Sebastian Rochi both flourished in 1620; the former lived in Padua, the latter in Venice. Georg Sella alla Stella lived in Venice in 1624. Michael Hartung lived in

1624 in Padua. This Hartung apprenticed in Venice with the quite young Leonhard Tieffenbrucker, who also did very fine work that almost compares with that of Vendelino Tieffenbrucker. Matthaeus Epp lived in Strasbourg, built wide-ribbed instruments, and made some lutes out of ivory.

Among the later masters who earned great renown in Germany, Herr Joachim Tielke of Hamburg deserves special mention. Lutes of his have been seen that have bodies built of pure ivory and ebony and necks very artfully inlaid with gold, silver, and mother-of-pearl. He was also skillful in his woodworking, and his instruments sound not particularly strong, but quite delicate and pleasant.

Herr Martin Hoffmann, who lived in Leipzig and was famous in some places for his work, passed away some years ago. However, this loss is replaced by his two surviving sons, of whom the younger has applied himself to violin and gamba making; but the elder, Herr Johann Christian Hoffmann, to lute building. This skillful master [Johann Christian] has earned himself such esteem in the *galant* world with his fine work that his lutes have primarily been sent to Holland, England, and France. It is worthy of special note that in the building of his lutes he not only creates great proportionate beauty, but also a good and pure tone. In the building of lute necks he has surpassed his father, for he makes them to fit the hand of each owner, whereas his father's usually turned out a bit too thick. He also knows how to place the courses and strings at the proper distances so that his lutes can be manipulated very easily. Herr Schmid, also resident in Leipzig, was an apprentice of his.

In Vienna, Herr Andreas Bähr and Herr Matthaeus Fux, both famous lute makers, are well known. The former built with wide staves and his instruments enjoyed uncommon esteem with the famous Count Losy. The latter also built good lutes and violins and was employed at the Imperial Court.

Thomas and Joseph Edlinger, father and son, have distinguished themselves in Prague. The latter was in Italy for a considerable time, so we can expect good work from his hands. Before him, there was a Martin Schott, also in Prague, who was very famous for Roman theorboes, which he copied superbly. Sebastian Rauch also lived in Prague and worked with the famous Herr Schelle in Nuremberg.

Matthaeus Hummel in Nuremberg was the master of the previously mentioned Herr Schelle, who profited so well by him that he [Schelle] has distinguished himself with his reliable work in Italy and France as well as in Upper and Lower Germany and other cultivated parts of Europe. His lutes often turn out so well that the masters who get them from him for a fair price occasionally have had the good luck, after the lutes have been broken in a bit, to sell them to connoisseurs and amateurs sometimes for a hundred and sometimes for sixty to seventy *Reichs-Thaler*. His instruments are of moderate size, built for almost everyone's hand, have a beautiful and accurate proportion in body and string arrangement, are shallow, wide-ribbed, oblong, and project the tone far into the distance. He has a large stock of all sorts of rare, dry, and beautiful wood best suited for instruments, and one can purchase his instruments with confidence.

The Breslau lutes are also not to be disdained. Michael Stürtzer concentrated as much on decoration as good tone, but Johann Michael Güttler worked primarily on powerful volume.

Every worthy friend of the lute can select a master here who may best satisfy him, because this depends most appropriately upon individual taste. If some should be missing who can be counted among the famous people, I will not neglect to mention them at another opportunity when I have assembled more information about them. For now, I ask that the reader be content with the names and the achievements of the famous masters mentioned here.

PART II

Theory and Practice

CHAPTER I

The prejudices that are held against the lute

BEFORE we can achieve understanding, it will be necessary to turn our attention to the prejudices by which this otherwise noble instrument has unnecessarily been made unpopular. Of them, three appear here:
1. The frequent and annoying tuning.
2. The imperfection and consequent illusion of difficulty.
3. The exorbitant cost of keeping the instrument strung.

Herr Mattheson quite innocently allowed himself to be deceived by these three main prejudices. Before I undertake to dissect piece by piece what he says to the detriment of the lute in his *Neu-Eröffnetes Orchestre*, it is appropriate to report the causes that led him astray. In his *Critica Musica*, Part IV, page 280, he wrote:

> When I first heard a lutenist, who was a handsome and elegant cavalier, I tore all the strings from my harpsichord and only wanted to play the lute. I scratched upon it for quite awhile and thought nothing could be finer. But as I gradually realized the imperfection and inconvenience of the instrument my admiration abated considerably.

This is indeed a very elegant text, written with extraordinary understanding! He admits that in the beginning he was very excited about the hot cookies, but when he had to apply a little effort and constant diligence, which he calls inconvenience, he grew weary of it. He entrusts scratching upon the lute to his skilled hand alone, yet since, on the contrary, others have their innocent pleasure playing it, and because he could not excel as soon as he would have liked, he thinks that this was due to the lute's imperfection. Certainly an admirable thought! Not so fast, my friend! Not so fast. A man must have a composed mind with all things; he must examine his strengths and weaknesses, and must not attempt to fly until he has the feathers. Erudition and other noble arts and sciences require motivation, time, effort, constancy, and patience, even though the children of Lübeck are seen in Germany as seldom as the phoenix in Egypt, as Tacitus says in *The Annals,* Book VI.

Among many thousand teachers not one is so soon successful as the excellent and learned Silesian von Adel, who instructs a child in such a way as to bring him in a short time to an increasing growth in good and beautiful things. Since the time when Hippias and Bottifanga lived I cannot recall, as seriously as I lay the index finger of my right hand on my brow, that the kind of genius that Morhoff quite civilly mentions has been seen again.[ax] Respect always springs from a rare goodness and beauty of things, which is supported with general approval. Hate of the good stems either from inability to attain it or from great ignorance. From this, Herr Mattheson will see quite clearly how valid his contempt is and that it is easier to publish something than to prove it with solid reasons.

However, because he wants to master this art like the shoemaker wanted to master Apelles and has fluttered around out of his field with his satirical thoughts, I will see how I shall comport myself with such a great man, who is an arch-satyr, only that he lacks the large goatee, horns, long ears, and the hooves. I can already see in my mind how he throws his Latin grenades at my head. I hear him shouting with his ghastly voice: "Bring the lamps, torches, tallow, and lanterns! See Part 1 of *Critica Musica,* so that I can see who is trying to disturb me, the invincible Nospomanatamus, in my circles."[23]

Here I can do nothing more than recommend myself to Horace's "high *probates aes triplex circa pectus,*"[24] because I will take the liberty of modestly examining Herr Mattheson's further judgment of the lute. "The flattering lutes," he writes, "really have more partisans in the world than they merit, and their players are so unfortunate that when they can scratch out a few allemandes in the Viennese or Parisian style, they ask not a whit about real musical knowledge but are quite satisfied with their poverty."

Qui bene distinquit bene docet.[25] Herr Mattheson, however, did not take heed of this. The Viennese style of playing the lute consists of taking the beautiful and distinctive qualities that other great masters there have in their music and applying them to the lute. But the French, as already shown above, seldom have free and ingenious melodies in their lute pieces. They brush chords with their fingers as if they were scratching and have stood by their French taste without any other instruction. The Viennese, however, only choose what is most beautiful. Therefore everything cannot be lumped together but rather must be differentiated.

He called the lute "flattering," to express its nature with

---

23. Baron is satirizing Mattheson with the latter's own words, from page 5 of *Critica Musica.*
24. "Three-fold bronze around the chest."
25. Who can distinguish well teaches well.

this participle. Flattery is the undeserved praise of something by someone who is furthering his own self-interest. But it only applies to animals, not to lifeless creatures. That this noble instrument can easily endear itself, especially to civilized dispositions, stems from the fact that it exceeds many others in delicacy.

When he says like the Delphic oracle that all *professores* (who are people that excel in this genre) put aside all musical and real sciences, he has deceived himself in this opinion like the *malade imaginaire* of Moliere. For I have already shown above how the earliest masters strove to imitate other composers and to be inventive themselves.

Mattheson proceeds further with his reasoning and says: "Some are so conceited as to call themselves composers, although they have truly not learned what consonance and dissonance are." Oh hold the horses, otherwise Hans will buck! I would be very curious to see a lute composer who had learned neither through nature nor art what the difference between consonance and dissonance is. Chords are just like many men who ingratiate themselves with everybody quite easily, but this quickly won favor cannot be ascribed to their merits. A man who has let himself become soured on the world should first find a friend who can absorb something uniform from everyone's temperament and apply the trust that others grant him to his goal.

Consonances have in their proportionate accord just such a relation and sympathy with human nature, without having to introduce themselves through a spokesman. Dissonances, however, are in themselves repulsive and contrary to human nature if they are not immediately resolved or changed into consonances, despite the fact that either can have an extraordinary effect when placed at the right spot. Now because music and the rules of composition are derived from hearing and harmony, not hearing from music, a genius who is so inclined and who plays harpsichord or lute well, especially when he has heard much good music besides, is able to compose something pleasant in the appropriate fashion. He does not need to understand what *hypate, parhypate, lychanos, mese, prolambanomenos,* and *hypatehypaton* are. Although composition comes as naturally to some people as verses flow from some poets, there are nevertheless fundamentals of composition unknown to those who compose or poetize by much practice and for which they can give no reason. It requires a deft, resolute, lively, and fiery mind and a healthy imagination to conceive all effects and beauties of music.

I can still clearly recall what one of the most learned and theoretically experienced *Kapellmeister* once said to me in a long discussion. He said it is better in such matters to follow natural inclination first, and later, after having seen and heard enough and become practiced, the composer might well apply himself to speculative things, but rationally, for too much speculative theory, since it is too diverting, only distracts him from his true character and leads him to constraint.

In my experience the overly artificial and correct composition, in which there is neither spirit, nor fire, nor the so-called *je ne sais quoi,* has earned little or no applause. My attitude here is not to disdain the theoretical and speculative rules and terms of art, because I occupy myself daily with investigation of them, as far as my affairs permit. Rather I recommend that they be used with discretion, for few today contribute anything to actual practice. Most are only of value for knowledge and historical study, since all rules of art, except for those founded in nature itself, change with fashion just as clothes do.

Herr Mattheson's next argument is even better: "Those concerned should take note of this. I am not talking about skilled people here, and I respect everyone's abilities. However, what cannot be tolerated is when the ass is looked upon as the miller."

Here he exposes himself, as if he had his sights only on an anonymous person. After he has scolded enough, which he carries on further with much umbrage, suddenly the duty of natural law occurs to him, namely not to blame or damage anyone. Soon after, he again begins (in a manner not common among cultivated and respectable people) to rail against those who have an innocent inclination to our incomparable instrument. He makes a very ingenious comparison between the miller and the ass, by which the *tertium comparationis*[26] is just as appropriate as chaff in biscuit dough.

Now I would like to ask modestly every impartial, reasonable person whether or not Herr Mattheson is as well suited to judge the lute as the hare is to catch mice? There is something more to it than a few disordered thoughts, nervously slapped together, which fit as accurately as the many colors and threadbare spots on a well-trimmed beggar's coat. Although he respects all who love this instrument, certainly no one will ask for his approval, for he is

---

26. In rhetoric, the *Tertium comparationis* is the element held in common by two objects being compared.

obligated by natural law to give it if a man actually has merit. I am of the opinion that if someone begins shouting without reason or consideration, he should be regarded as an Arcadian miller-chorister with his hoarse voice.

I merely wished to write this in general, so that Herr Mattheson might not take his thoughts for granted, although this could be viewed as a retort. Be that as it may, what I have here asserted to the contrary does not come at all from the soul of an injured man.[ay] However, because Herr Mattheson is intent on finding new truths and preaches strongly against sophomoric opinions in his *Critica Musica,* I cannot avoid considering some of the conclusions of his special, new-found logic. He cleverly concludes that there are a few, or perhaps only one, who achieve something good or great on the lute (now notice the conclusion), *ergo* all the others are worth nothing. I would only say here that all conclusions that proceed by inductive reasoning should be swept away with a Latin duster. Perhaps in addition to the above-mentioned cavalier he heard a clumsy dilettante who, before Herr Mattheson most graciously granted him an audience, promised more in the red than the black. It would have been reasonable to dismiss this person alone, but not to generalize in such violent expressions.

He becomes more subtle, as if he had escaped reading Duns Scotus and Petrus Lombardus in school, and concludes that because Titius or Cajus did not accomplish much on the lute, even though Herr Mattheson passed himself off as a lutenist, *ergo,* the instrument itself is imperfect. Now I would like to know how Herr Mattheson was able to make such a little bit of *Schmaltz* into a magnificat and, in cold blood, deduce our instrument's imperfection from the playing of a clumsy dilettante who has facility neither in his head nor his fingers, and to confuse the vices of an immature, unaccomplished player with the virtue of this innocent instrument.

If I should argue that Herr Handel in England and the famous *Kapellmeister* Bach in Leipzig play the clavichord, harpsichord, and organ far better than Herr Mattheson and compose more learned pieces that find far more approbation among music experts than do his, and that *ergo* neither Herr Mattheson's harpsichord playing nor his *Der Brauchbare Virtuose*[27] are worth anything at all, would that not be a curious conclusion? I am in favor of recognizing his accomplishments, because he is so kind as to recognize those of others.

He continues: "The insinuating sound of this deceitful instrument always promises more than it delivers, and before we know where its strength and weakness lies, we think that nothing more charming may be heard on earth, as I myself was deceived by this siren. But once we see through these pitiful artifices, all the lute's virtue vanishes immediately." Now we will get to the bottom of this awful and abominable deceit immediately. Deception refers to humans, and so a person only deceives himself when he thinks falsely, though the subject has presented itself clearly and should have been perceived according to its natural construction. But here it is necessary that the object be at a proper distance, that the air in between be well constituted, and lastly that the sensory organ with which the object is

---

27. Johann Mattheson, *Der Brauchbare Virtuose*, XII *Sonate per il Violino, overo Flauto traverso* [with basso continuo] (Hamburg, 1720).

to be perceived should have all its healthy requisites. Herr Mattheson should now consider whether he is capable of penetrating the delicate subject according to these principles. If he was deceived by the so-called siren, he has shown that he is no clever Ulysses, who could avoid all dangers. Descartes made a great deal of noise about deception of the senses, and although the objects presented themselves to him as by these or those attendant circumstances they should appear, no one can assert that he falsely affirmed or negated anything that would here be called deception.

Herr Mattheson does not know what strength and weakness on the lute are, for had he known their effect, he would have thought in more complimentary terms and not criticized it so severely. On the subject of the lute's virtue, it is certainly stained by the pitiful playing of clumsy duffers, but not nullified.

Before I go any further I must communicate to him a truth that was found valid a hundred and sixty-eight years ago. The above-mentioned Sebastian Ochsenkuhn recognized that ingenious intellect, in the manner of busy bees, could make a treasure of art and loveliness from a small, wooden box.[az] If we wished to conclude *a majori ad minus, ab imperfecto ad perfectius*,[28] as we should, what a surprise would result.

Now Herr Mattheson hits the nail on the head when he writes: "We pay twice for the best lute piece, for we have to hear the eternal tuning that goes with it. If a lutenist lives to be eighty years old, surely he has spent sixty years tuning. The worst of it is that among a hundred (especially

---

28. From the great to the small, from the incomplete to the more complete.

non-professionals), scarcely two are capable of tuning accurately. In addition, there is trouble with bad or spliced strings, especially the chanterelle, and trouble with frets and, tuning pegs, so that I have heard that it costs as much in Paris to keep a lute as it does a horse."

In this paragraph Herr Mattheson took great pains to vent his envy and hate in prejudicing everyone against this instrument, thus it is appropriate to set him straight. He complains that we pay double for the best lute piece, but he may be answered that it is easier to scare up twenty cartloads of other music than a dozen lute partitas that are worth something and are in good taste. Because rarity increases the value not only of diamonds and jewels but of other beautiful things as well, the friends of this worthy instrument would do well to reflect on this fact, since no one can levy taxes on it. A master can accept such overpayment *salva conscientia, quia quaevis donatio nullo cogente jure ex liberrima voluntate proficiscitur.*[29]

The annoying and wearisome tuning is not at all as Herr Mattheson has represented it. A master must be able to tune his instrument instantly while playing, so that it is scarcely heard, even when a peg has slipped. It also does not happen (except when an instrument has been newly strung and the strings have not yet sufficiently stretched) that all the strings are out of tune when it is taken out of the case. That there are: from time to time amateurs who cannot handle it very well is a flaw in their own nature, and this cannot detract from the instrument in the slightest, since there are

---

29. With a sure conscience, because any offering, in the absence of a compelling law, originates in one's freest will.

few of these people. If something is wrong with a peg, it can be cheaply replaced in a day and will last another fifty to sixty years. Herr Matthesson's mention of the occasional bad strings is like a legal case, and he should still vaguely recall a little juridicial huntsman's salute that says: *Casum fortuitum nemo praestat et nemini imputari debet.*[30]

The expense of maintaining the lute with strings is not at all true, let alone so precarious. Thus I think that the Parisian horses, if someone tried to maintain them for a year with two *Thalers'* worth of feed, would very shortly look like one of the seven scrawny, emaciated cows that the pharaoh saw in his dream. The chanterelles, as is well known, are sold in bundles and can be bought in some places for two *Gulden* and one *Reichs-Thaler,* or in Nuremberg for one *Gulden*. It has been mentioned that some strings will not hold at a pitch the instrument can otherwise take. This fate is common to all strings, and it sometimes happens that either the material they are made of or the weather is contrary. However, such infrequent occurrences are not to be seen as usual, chronic, and ordinary, and, as otherwise in life, the player must occasionally accept a small inconvenience for the sake of the greater good.

It is no great feat to abuse good, beautiful, and blameless things thoughtlessly with great and grandiloquent words. But to elevate mean things and to raise them, as it were, from the dust to the throne is a better sign of a great genius. Erasmus of Rotterdam amazed all clever people, for he knew how to praise folly in an ingenious manner. Brissonius

---

30. No one is superior to a chance mishap, and no one ought to be blamed.

and Scaliger write about the flea; Majoragius praised mud; Andreas Arnaudius praised Bacchus; Christophorus Hegendorphius, Geraldus Bucholdianus, and Robertus, a Jesuit, lauded drunkenness; Andreas Cotlerus extolled lust; Thrasimachus Carneades and Christophorus Neander exalted injustice almost to the stars; Thephanus Guazza flattered flattery; and Daniel Heinsius, in the oration that he addressed to the conscript fathers of the Mendicants, lauded the foul and loathsome louse as if it were the most beautiful animal on earth. Here Herr Mattheson can easily perceive that he is not to be counted among such penetrating minds, but rather among the windbags who, as Gracián says, make a thing worse than it actually is.[ba]

The misconception that is often heard today—namely that a lute must have as many strings as a horse must have feed—stems from the olden days and its first tuning. I showed above that after the first chanterelle was added, it was tuned to *Chorton* g'. But after the rise of musical theater and *Singspiel,* the *Kammerton* was invented in order to spare the breast and throat of the singer and the strings of the instrumentalist. Thus the lute was given an entirely different tuning, so that now the chanterelle, which caused the most vexation, is pitched at *Kammerton* f', and there are instances where a Roman string lasted four weeks.[31]

Now Herr Mattheson gets to really vile thoughts and says: "It would be best if each lutenist would carefully attend to his mistress, seeing if she could be taught to value tuning more than playing. Who knows that he might now

---

31. For a discussion of *Chorton* and *Kammerton* see Arthur Mendel, 'On the Pitches in use in Bach's time," *MQ*, Vol. XLI (1955), pp. 332–354 and 466–480.

and then succeed, and then he would have accomplished enough."

Herr Mattheson must have experimented more than too much with the good effect of music on women, for he brings in the fair sex here, although the subject is not apropos. Because, as it appears, he practiced this far more than the lute, he is often caught in the pleasant doubt whether to admire the ladies with humble love or with enamored humility. Whoever could produce such a curious invention as entertainment with tuning rather than melody should rightly be called Magnus Apollo. Herr Mattheson, a profound music theorist, must have exerted himself considerably to arrive at such an idea. If he succeeds at it, he should communicate it to others, because we should daily strive to perfect the arts.

A rational man will always behave respectfully in the presence of *galant* ladies, but not excessively so as our ancestors did in Tacitus' *De moribus Germanorum*, Chapter 8. Herr Mattheson comes even closer to the idea when he writes: "People say that after the one *qui a son Logis à l'Aigle*, a certain *Wise* lutenist is a perfect musician.[32] If so, I believe that such a person could do things on the lute at which the whole swarm of lute players would be amazed. A certain pretty woman here can sufficiently and astonishingly demonstrate that this is not impossible. Nonetheless, such virtue must be ascribed not so much to the rather deficient instrument as to the great diligence, judgment, and skill of those persons who produce such extraordinary things on it."

---

32. Mattheson is punning on the names of Count Losy (Logy) and Sylvius Leopold Weiss (Weis).

Here Herr Mattheson speaks of two masters, namely of one *qui a son Logis à l'Aigle* and of the famed Herr Weiss. He put the anonymous master in order before Herr Weiss and did not think of the old school rule, *quod a potiori fiat denominatio*.[33] That profundity alone in music should make a perfect master seems as absurd to me as though sine and mean had been confused. It is incontestably true that if a man has the necessary natural requisites for the instrument and also applies himself to the study of music and composition, he will be successful. However, it certainly cannot be said that understanding of music contributes anything to manual dexterity, otherwise Herr Mattheson would doubtless be one of the finest masters of the lute, although he tacitly admits his lack of skill. It is not at all necessary to smear those who love this instrument with such abusive, awful, and barbaric terms, because it is an innocent matter whether many or few play it.

In the fifth century, as is known, the Vandals, Visigoths, Ostrogoths, Huns, Alamanni, Svevi, Burgundians, Rugi, Heruli, Lombards, and Franks invaded the Roman and German provinces in swarms (as is written in the old German chronicles). However, I know nothing about the violence of those who play the lute, unless of course they be courageous enough to create complete disorder with Herr Mattheson's ideas (to which there was already an inclination before I began to write), chase after those that fled, and club them in the back as the Polish do. I will further instruct him elsewhere, which will be supernaturally astonishing.

Herr Mattheson introduces a new fashion of citing

---

33. Let what is better be the denomination.

authorities. Whereas previously one scholar referred to another, he refers to a pretty woman. Yet I think that she has more taste and understanding for *galant* things than he himself, for she truthfully reports to him what can be attained by no other means than good insight. He considers the instrument to be imperfect by nature and attributes playing, potential, and intrinsic quality of the instrument only to the masters, whereas the possibility must be inherent in the thing itself (that a person begins to study). Scholars attribute the *supernaturalia* only to the highest God, the *praeternaturalia* (beyond the natural) to the spirits, and *possibilitatem naturalem* (natural ability) only to men and objects. He is so orderly in his reasoning that he often does not know himself what he is writing, for he puts affirmative and negative in front of the same thing without differentiation. At first he asserted that judgment, great diligence, and skill could make something perfect out of an imperfect thing; later he affirms the imperfection of the lute, and again denies that perfect things could be played on it, although he had originally asserted this. He limps along and says: "For if the instrument were perfect, it would be no miracle that perfect things were played on it."

He has no conception of perfection of things in general nor of his particular kind of perfection. Concerning the former, it is *"affectio entis existentis, cui omnia essentialia et accidentalia naturaliter ita sunt uniti, ut ejus duratio et hominis bonum et finis ad illud tendens junctis viribus possibiliter promoveri possit."*[34] But the other type of

---

34. "The tendency of an existing being, in whom all essentials and accidentals are so naturally united that its continuance, the good of man and the end to which it tends, in common with mankind, can be promoted."

perfection that is considered here occurs when the essential parts of a thing are present and only some dispensable accidentals are absent.

Let us compare the keyboard, which is the mother of all harmony, and the lute to demonstrate for the sly and cunning Herr Mattheson that possibilities must exist not only in the instrument but in the master as well, and that everything happens without sorcery. To reach this goal it will be necessary to examine, after music, the fingerboard (which the French call *la manche)* to show what can be done upon it. As a better illustration I will put down its range, so that not only the double and triple unisons, but also the many octaves with their appropriate semitones can clearly be recognized. This is the range of an eleven-course lute. There is also one with thirteen courses, whereby the eleventh course still lies over the fingerboard, so that almost the complete scale up to c''' exists, as on the keyboard.

99

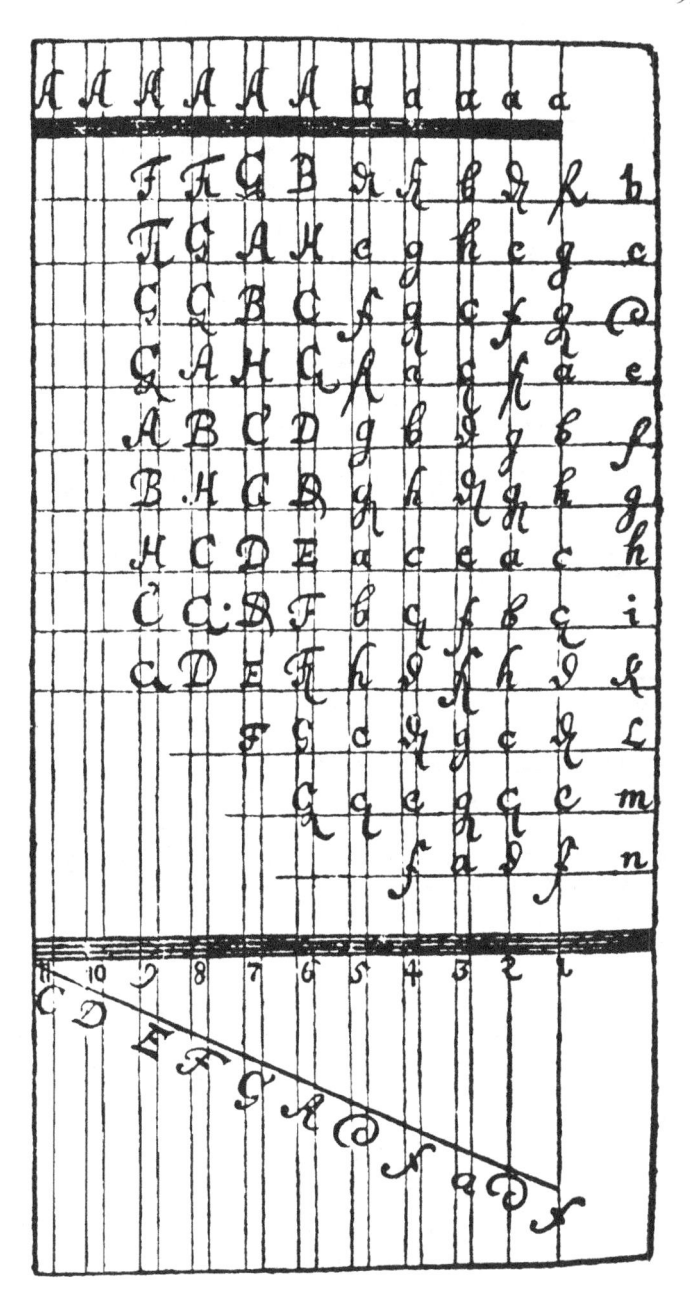

100

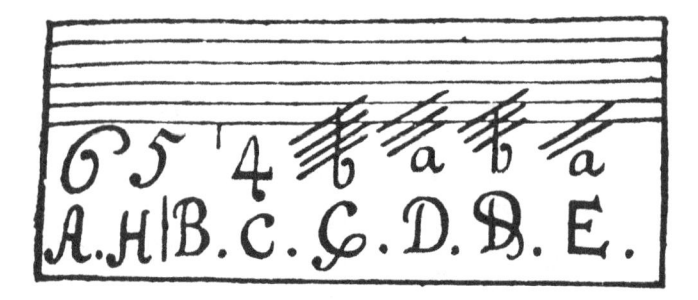

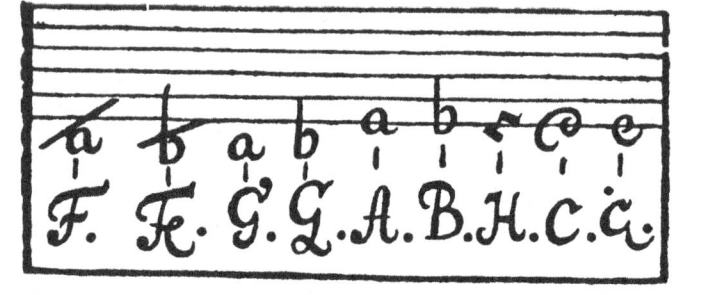

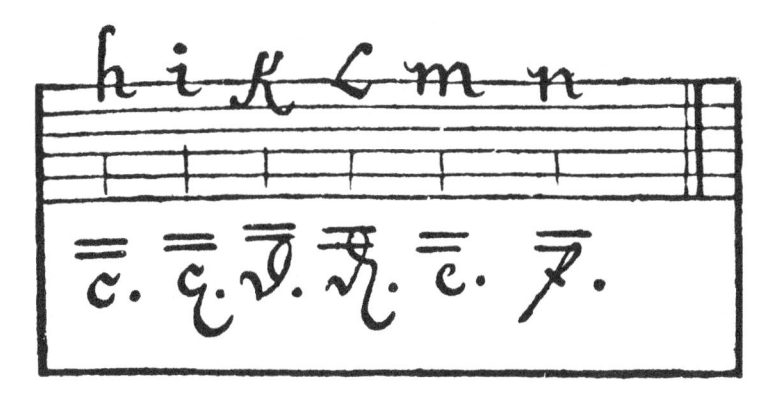

Although here in the high range some tones are lacking, they can be played by octave displacement. If desired, the range can be extended to c''' and even further by adjusting the neck,[35] for these things are subject to the judgment of everyone, and even without them enough can be done on the lute to delight everyone.

In addition all semitones are easily available, even double and triple unisons. The triad is not only available without constraint, but it can also be strengthened by arpeggiating as on the keyboard, as the following example demonstrates.

---

35. Since the open first string is the pitch f', the normal high note would be twelve frets higher or f''. The common configuration for the Baroque lute in Baron's time was nine gut frets tied on the neck, and two or three hardwood frets glued onto the belly. It is difficult to guess what Baron means by "adjusting the neck" (*so dörffte nur der Hals darnach eingerichtet werden*) to add another perfect fifth to the range.

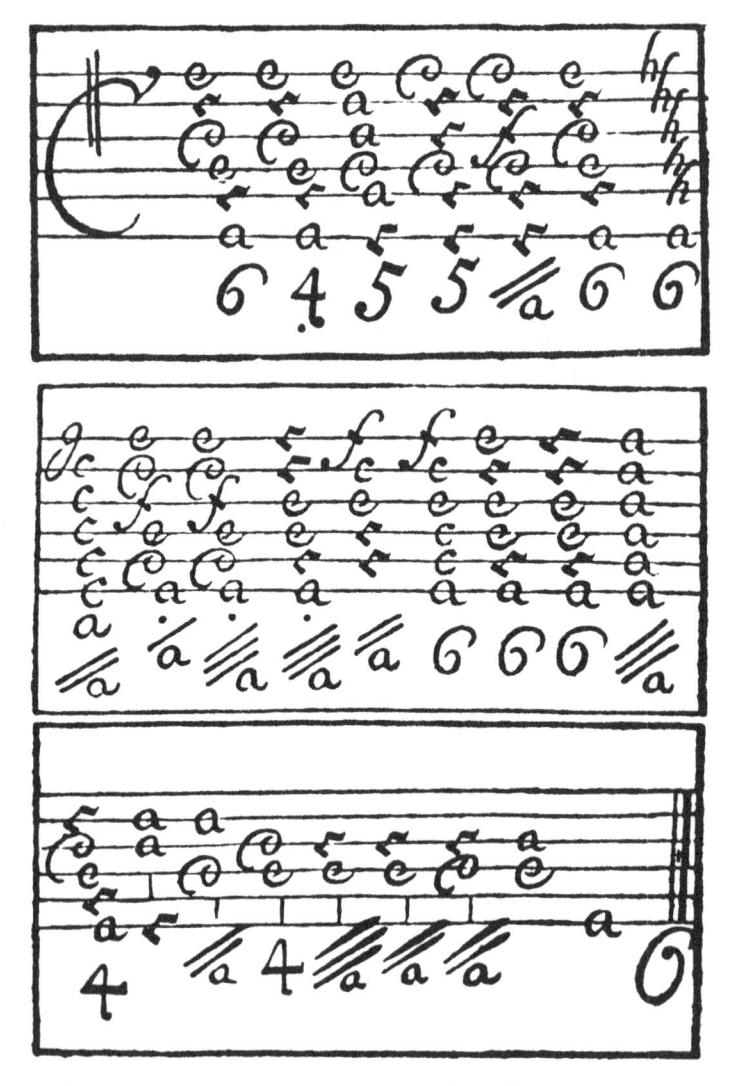

The transcription of this example is found on page 108.

Now if Herr Mattheson would interject that many tones can be played simultaneously in the bass on the keyboard, this is not necessary, because the triad must not lie only in the bass, but rather in the bass, middle, and upper voices. If he would say further that it is not possible on the lute to play difficult, springing basses as quickly as a simultaneous melody in the high range, especially in *Galanterie* pieces, it suffices to inform him that delicacy depends more upon the spirit in the composition and in the beautiful expressions of the master than on difficulty. Difficulty can be introduced at other points.

The lutenist can strike a chord very strongly and allow the tone to die away imperceptibly while arpeggiating, so that it becomes first louder, then softer, which cannot be done on the harpsichord without great affectation, since the player must hop from one keyboard to the other. Indeed, I already mentioned above that our instrument has many tones doubly and triply, which has a special effect in many cases. Further, the lute can very conveniently be carried along on trips. The player can even walk back and forth in a room with it, playing the loveliest passages and harmonies, which can be done neither with the clavichord nor the harpsichord.

Thus Herr Mattheson can see what his kind of imperfection is, and how sometimes two things are alike and sometimes one has a special effect that the other does not. It is important not to be like the shepherd who can only praise his own staff, as Herr Mattheson has done, because there are some people who, like peasants, believe everything that is printed without taking the trouble to examine the reasoning.

Now I would like to know what friendly spirit fooled Herr Mattheson into thinking that his pleasant, twanging harp of David is more suited to full accompaniment than the lute. In Silesia and Bohemia the debauched Catholic students often march around in the taverns, which we do not hear of lutenists. This harp has not a single chromatic tone, and if it can accompany anything it would be a drinking song. No artful harmonies can be played on it, because there is not a single chromatic key to be heard or seen on it. And if there were someone who could conjure them up while playing, I think that the whole swarm of keyboard players would be amazed, especially their prince, Herr Mattheson, who wants to put everyone to the test, *ut salvo honore et pace tua lector benevole ipsius terminis utar*.[36] In his description this harp has strings made of meat, but he does not indicate whether they are of *Knackwurst* or beef. I will leave this to the reader's profound contemplation.

He teaches further, saying: "Formerly the Italians liked to accompany and play thoroughbass on the lute, but since the theorbo has come into use, they gladly bid farewell to the lute. In churches and operas, the feigned accompaniment of the lute is lousy and serves more to give airs to the instrument than aid to the singer, for which the accompaniment of the colascione is more suitable. What can be accomplished with thoroughbass in chamber music on the lute may well be fine, if it could only be heard."

Here Herr Mattheson makes a great effort to prove that the accompaniment on the lute was discarded *tout à fait* by the Italians. However, he does not have the slightest knowledge about the theorbo. Since he read Pater [Anastasius] Kircher, I am surprised that he did not notice that this instrument was made out of the lute by a Neapolitan charlatan

---

36. So that, with my honor and your good will intact, benevolent reader, I might use the terms of this man.

(*Markt-Schreier*), who named the instrument after a vessel in which he prepared his mess. Afterwards, when its usefulness had been recognized, it was cultivated and ennobled by a German nobleman named Hieronymus Kapsberger, who was a fine musician.[bb]

We can say that the theorbo is louder, but that the lute is all the more delicate. Herr Mattheson did not consider in this case that eagles could be born of ravens. Here he can see that the famous Kircher is not of one mind with him, for he not only prefers this instrument to others but demonstrates that all three types are perfect and that variations and decorations can be added to them. The best and most beautiful theorboes used to be made in Rome and Padua. The Roman ones, also called chitarrones, were the largest, measuring seven feet, two inches in length.

Now because Pater Kircher considers the theorbo a daughter of the lute, as is quite proper, the author of the *Edelmann* is even more in the right when he considers Boethius the first lute maker and lutenist, for even Kircher says that the lute, mandora, and guitar are essentially the same, since they only differ in number of strings and tuning.[bc] But the other instruments that are now seldom used because of their imperfect nature, for instance the quinterna or chiterna, pandurina or little mandor, benorcon, orpharion, citharra, and so forth, are correctly described by Kircher,[bd] who says that it would be indecent for a rational musician to have anything to do with them, for he can take up something more useful and praiseworthy in music.

The Paduan theorboes were more convenient to handle and only measured five feet in length. Because the Roman archlutes were not so well suited to harmony, since they had only six single strings on the fingerboard, the Paduan ones were given eight single courses or strings. The theorbo's tuning was the same as the old lute tuning: **g' d' a f c G F E D C B'** (or **Bb'**) **A' G' F' E' D'**. Today, however, it commonly has the new lute tuning, which our own lute still has, because it was too much trouble for the lutenist to have to suddenly rethink everything when he picked up the old theorbo. Today the theorboes also have double courses, except for the basses, which are stretched freely from the bridge to the second pegbox. From this Herr Mattheson can see first that the theorbo and lute have never differed except with respect to their size and range, and secondly that the lute, because of its delicacy, serves well in trios or other chamber music with few participants. The theorbo, because of its power, serves best in groups of thirty to forty musicians, as in churches and operas.

From his further manner of writing we can see without any large Spanish spectacles that Herr Mattheson is a very polite gentleman, for he gallantly describes the accompaniment of the lute in such places as "lousy," although it does not belong there at all. If he behaves in rational society as he does in writing, he must be able to introduce himself beautifully with his messenger-boy philosophy. All things can be appropriate at the proper time, place, or other circumstances. It would be the greatest folly to take a little clavichord, or even the largest harpsichord, perfect as it is in harmony, and attempt to keep the congregation in the cathedral in Milan or at Saint Peter's in Rome on the melody as the organ can. It does not follow that such a beautiful and lovely instrument must be scorned because it does not do sufficient service in churches and operas, for

Herr Mattheson would otherwise have to condemn many other things.

He says that the colascione is much more useful in accompaniments but forgets that it is only the bass of a lute, and could not be more than the whole instrument, especially since it is quite reasonable that more can be done with many strings than with three, four, or six courses. But it is a fault in his nature that he was not able to perceive the special delicacy in chamber music accompaniment with the lute, and he should not ascribe it to the instrument, and should shout "Enough" another time.

I would not ordinarily have ventured to say anything that would concern Herr Mattheson. But since I found that he does not produce anything of the slightest probability, I could not allow his opinion on this subject to go unchallenged. Moreover, he appealed to Sempronius and Sylvia, thus he is innerly convinced that inevitability would not have suffered it otherwise. My task is not to criticize all sorts of petty things, for I have always held that the best rule is to think only of the virtues and not the faults of good people, just as Vespasianus did in Tacitus.[be] However, because untruth teaches people misconceptions that ruin the mind, and arts and sciences too, and that oppress without need or cause, I have considered all this necessary, for disciplines should be explained and made clear.

If he calls all lights and lamps together to illuminate my principles, I, on the contrary, will ask Herr Diogenes for his lantern. If he should wonder that a little light shimmers even in dark corners, he should remember that in Cicero's grave lights were found that had long burned without being cleaned, and that he has not grasped healthy reason ahead of other men all by himself. Enough for now.

Transcription of the example on page 102.

CHAPTER II

Genius on the Lute

Now that the fashionable misconceptions have been clearly swept away in the preceding chapter, I hope it will be appropriate to raise the question of which genius (*Genie*) is best suited to the lute. To thoroughly answer this question, it will be necessary to observe the goals of two types of people. There are some who wish to excel, and who demand something more. Some others, however, are merely amateurs who undertake the noble exercise only for their peace of mind. Now because this is a discipline that is perceived with the most senses, it tries them to the fullest. The profound Spaniard Gracián [Baltasar Gracián y Morales], describing a complete soul, says the following in his *El discreto*, Chapter 1: "If a man is missing one of his five senses, much of his life is missing, and his soul is lamed, as it were."

Although normally only three senses, namely sight, hearing, and feeling, are called upon in music, the remaining ones do no harm, especially if they contribute something to natural human perfection. Because all things, before reason can judge them and apply them to a goal, must first fall upon the external senses, Gracián is absolutely right when he calls such a flaw a laming, especially when we consider that our spiritual powers would be hindered in perceiving the character of a given thing if a sense necessary to the perception were lacking. Concerning sight, it is more than well known to what extent we perceive and imagine external signs such as tablature with it. The imagination communicates its meaning to the life spirits, which bring it through nerves and muscles to the hands. If the written chord has been fingered, it must be delivered by subtle and healthy hearing to the rational soul, which is distinguished by its power of decision, and which must then pass judgment on the concord or discord. The sooner such a perception of ideas occurs, the finer and more fiery is the spirit and character. Therefore the famous Dr. Andreas Rüdiger of Leipzig defended this concept cleverly against the famous mechanicians, Cartesians, Cronium, and Willisium and against those who wanted to introduce *motum successivum*. As support for his expertise he primarily cited famous lutenists as examples.[bf]

Many learned people even assert that far more is demanded to become a good lutenist than another type of musician — a question I will not judge. It is certainly true that it is one of the most acute instruments, just as chess is among other games. Thus it has been cultivated so often by eminent and learned people. Because quick perception enables one who enlists the aid of constancy of purpose to climb over the highest mountains of difficulty, something special and excellent must necessarily happen to people who have the above-mentioned prerequisites. Among these geniuses our Herr Weiss and other great virtuosi can be counted.

However, another type of person does not ordain great powers of reason to music, but rather ascribes everything to sound hearing. He errs to such an extent that he is handing someone the sword, as it were, with which to whack his knots of doubt in two. The soul is a queen who keeps court in the palace of the human heart. The external senses are her servants, who report to her the representations of all objects and await her judgment. How can the messenger be better than the ruler?

To relieve such people of their misconceptions, we shall observe what music has to deal with: it invents, judges, and practices. If a person wishes to invent something, he must be provided with a good ingenuity. Every invention is itself like gold ore, which must be cleansed of its dross, and judgment must be the cleanser. It must distinguish good from bad melodies and be able to select the best. If someone sets two or more voices, he must judge exactly how the proportions relate to each other, so that not only the intended affect but also a suitable melody emerges. He must know the strengths and weaknesses of those who will perform his pieces, for it sometimes happens that the composition is good but the performance is bad. He must also reflect on the range of the instruments, so that the melody does not emerge unnaturally but rather flows out. Other things will remain unsaid.

Because such a person thinks of these kinds of things, which always have certain truths as their foundation, one can say nothing more than that these things are necessary. For the recognition of truth, no matter what it consists of, is primarily the province of reason. There are also some who ascribe all art and skill to the fingers alone, and some are even afraid to learn to play the lute or other musical instruments because they think their fingers are too short or too thick.

At this point a story occurs to me that is well suited to illustrate our purpose. A certain bad and not very smart lutenist (whom I will call Marcolphus von Butterchurn) once traveled to one of the most splendid and *galant* courts in Germany in order to display his not very great skill with strange dexterity. When he announced himself to the *Kapellmeister*, as is customary, he was told that he could do so on the condition that he first play for the *Kapellmeister*, so that the latter might then be able to give an exact account of it to his sovereign. When he had done so to very slight applause, the *Kapellmeister* praised him notwithstanding and promised that he would in time send someone for him to instruct while he stayed in Bellinde,[37] so that he would have some diversion before he had his audience.

There was at that same court a very fine, retired lutenist who privately wore clothes in which Marcolphus thought him a cavalier. The *Kapellmeister* invited this old lutenist to meet Marcolphus, for they had agreed that Cleontes, as he was called, would pass himself off to Marcolphus as a prospective student. Now the former again displayed his skill and the latter acted as if he especially admired it and requested that he might be so kind as to give him lessons. Before Marcolphus would agree, Cleontes had to show him his fingers, which Marcolphus judged to be rather inept. The old man could scarcely contain his laughter, but the lesson began. Cleontes kept his pretense for quite awhile and stumbled very slowly through the first easy piece like a beginner, but suddenly he dispersed the smoke and proved to Marcolphus that not inept, ungainly fingers, but rather a bright and clever mind is the decisive factor. When poor Marcolphus became aware of this, to his great consternation,

---

37. The term "Bellinde" has defied translation and deciphering.

as will easily be imagined, all desire for an audience disappeared. After he excused himself, he boarded the mail coach and traveled merrily home.

The practice or execution of music occurs in two ways. The first consists of playing the notes and melody just as they are written on the paper, with no concern for *galant* additions that will press upon the emotions. This method we will leave to the "artists of the lowest caliber," as Kircher says. This manner is simple, noisy, and affects only common and uncultivated temperaments, thus it is out of place at court.

The other manner of playing is the correct one, and it can quite properly be called oratory. I call it this because it agrees with the chief goal of rhetoric. If we observe the qualities of a good orator, we will find that his achievement consists of the following: the elegance of his words; the loftiness and merit of his thoughts and subjects; and the persuasion and emotion of the affects. A virtuoso musician must possess all of these qualities.

Elegance will be discussed below; now expression of the melodies will be treated. By the stroke, attack, and touch, the right weight is given. For after the tone is produced and is presented wavering, strongly, weakly, stronger, weaker to the ear, then occurs the communication to the emotions, which are thus moved. This manner of playing belongs only to virtuosi and cannot be achieved without great attention and judgment. All disciplines require equal intelligence, and when someone possesses somewhat less of it, he can of course achieve his goal for his own diversion, but not on an absolute scale of excellence. It is certainly true that of all the senses, hearing has the most sensation of music, but I do not believe that it constitutes anything more. To not exceed the proper boundaries, I will consider the other type of people who want to learn music and particularly the lute for their pleasure, without the intent of achieving a great feat.

These people, although they lack by nature one thing or another that a solid musician requires, can nonetheless learn enough to be able to entertain themselves and others with all sorts of good suites. For them it is not necessary to have the things mentioned above present to an exceptional degree. It is enough if they have a good ear and memory. With the former, they hear high and low pitches or *proportion*, and with the other, they easily grasp and retain the melodies, which helps them get a piece quickly into their fingers. Those who lack both of these qualities, even though they have a great desire to learn, will never accomplish anything, try as they might, *quia non cuilibet licet adire Corinthum*.[38] Yet there are also people in whom the senses and powers of the soul are sometimes asleep, as it were, and who, because of lack of exposure to culture, do not know for what they are suited, since they were never placed in a position where they had to act. Others try to offset their natural deficiencies with great, painstaking diligence, thinking as Horace does: *"Perrupit Acheronta Herculeus labor/Nil mortalibus arduum est."*[39] These people sometimes accomplish something. But usually, because they have to force the invitation of Minerva too hard, they grow weary of it and are often so simple as to ascribe their

---

38. Because not every man can go to Corinth.
39. "The effort of Hercules overcame Acheron/Nothing is difficult for mortals to attain."

innate ineptitude either to the instructor or to the difficulty of the instrument, although they pick up other things readily. Very few are totally unfit for music, for the ideal of this noble art is inborn in almost everyone. God and nature must do the best with our knowledge.

The rules of art are weak means with which we come to the aid of our corrupted souls. They usually arose from experience and were invented from what was practiced most. They are only kindling that ignites the fire of the mind and temperament. They say and command what we should do. If a person has the ability to obey their commands, he will reach his goal all the sooner.

Today the lute has been made so easy that even children of seven or eight years can learn something on it. I can truthfully report that the son of an eminent Breslau merchant named Kropfganss, who was this age, already played very fine suites on the lute. Although his instructor, named Seeliger, made a great effort to win a larger reputation through this student, the undertaking was interrupted by his untimely death. This loss was replaced by his brother, however, so that the child, now in his more mature years, has a great *profectus* (profit).

For my part, I shall leave all that I have said about genius to everyone's scrutiny and judgment. I can contribute nothing more to the subject for now.

CHAPTER III

The Fundamentals of the Instrument: Posture, Positioning of the Hands, New Tablature, Fingering

Now that genius has been examined, we must get to the heart of the matter and consider the beginning stages of lute playing. Herr Mattheson will laugh at me as Pluto does for wanting to introduce and understand the deportment that he satirizes. It will suffice to say that two important motives have moved me to this, namely the ugly grimaces that many wear while playing their instrument, and the position and posture of a lutenist, for if he is not secure in them he will hardly be able to progress.

On the subject of grimaces, I knew someone myself who was fairly proficient on the viola da gamba, but who made such perilous and peculiar gestures that anyone who heard him felt pleasure, but seeing him was seized with fear, losing hearing and sight. For when he bowed up to the left, he drew his eyes and mouth after, and when he stroked back with the bow, he drew his eyes and mouth back too. When he made a rapid motion or trill, his whole face—eyes, nose, mouth, and cheeks—was in such rapid movement as if a secret war had broken out among the parts, or it abated as if he were a Quaker inspired by the Spirit.

Should not such a person assume a better and more

respectable demeanor? I believe so, namely one that consists of a modest indifference without affectation, so that it would have a grave or light effect. Decorum must be observed in all things, especially with the lute. For when a person shows his skill in the presence of eminent or other people and gesticulates in an unseemly manner, they will lose their appetite at such a spectacle. Ugly and indecorous gestures undo all that art or skill accomplishes.

With respect to posture of the body as well as of the hands, it is necessary to sit somewhat toward the left and press the instrument to the breast with the right hand. The thumb of the left hand and the little finger of the right contribute the most to securing the lute. For with the thumb, the lute is pressed forward onto the table; the right little finger must be placed by the chanterelle[bg] or thinnest string behind the bridge where it is held slightly curved, and the lute rests somewhat on the right thigh. The thumb of the left hand must always be held in the middle of the back of the neck, so that the player will not touch the upper strings with the fingers, which must not rest on the edge of the neck but must be held away from it. The hand is curved and the arm held well away from the body. The fingers are suspended separated over the fingerboard so that they do not accidentally touch the strings. The right or lower hand, as I will call it, must also be arched and the fingers held curved and apart, because they are hindered in motion if held close together. The thumb must always remain outstretched so that it can easily reach the basses.

As to the question of where to strike the strings of the lute so that the tone will be powerful enough, it will serve to know that this must be in the center of the space between the rose and the bridge, for there the contact will have the greatest effect. The further toward the fingerboard the strings are struck with the right hand, the softer and weaker will be the tone—it will lose power, so to speak. However, the player can certainly also move back and forth, once he has the necessary skill, when he wishes to change [the tone] and express something. Those still in the beginning stages will not be able to do this, for such variation demands considerable assurance.

When the posture is correct and has become more or less natural, the tyro must be taught knowledge of tablature and the strings. Tablature is today very easy to understand, because it no longer has any of the many annoying details about which the old composers, especially the two Newsidlers, made a great fuss. Its essence consists not of notes, as with other instruments, but rather of Latin longhand letters, arranged according to the alphabet. In all, there are six lines, to better and more easily distinguish the several courses. The mockery of Herr Mattheson in Chapter II, page 66 of his *[Neu-Eröffnetes] Orchestre*[bh] is as inappropriate as covering a blind eye with the hand, for it would be just as preposterous to assert that a dot would have been better than a whole line, or a minus clearer than a plus.

I, for my part, and with me all rational people, will find nothing absurd in the system of six lines, especially when we look at the nature of the instrument. We need no profound and melancholy critique when we consider, as already mentioned, the many courses that are all denoted by the upper six lines with small strokes for the basses. The reason that all *Galanterie* pieces (concertos, suites, and so forth) are not set in conventional notation but rather in tablature is that in tablature unisons are most readily distinguishable, which does not work with the signs common to other instruments, although a master [of the lute] must also have a command of these.

For example, the chanterelle is the first *a* and is the musical note **f'**, the *d* on the next course is also an **f'**, and the *i* on the third course sounds just like the first *a* and second *d*, so that according to mathematical proportions all three unisons are the same tone. These three unisons can be conveniently distinguished with different letters, since the player then knows where he should place his fingers.

If we were to take conventional notation for beginners and set pieces in it, it would be impossible for the amateur to guess which of these three he should select, and whether he should move his hand up or down the neck. The nature of other instruments admits no superfluities, because they are not necessary as they are here; thus the indication always remains on one spot, and all three unisons can be included in this one note.[40]

---

40. The notation is an octave higher than actual pitch.

If the reader, especially the amateur, is to have a clear idea of lute tablature, we must first distinguish the tones represented by the open courses as they appear on a common eleven-course lute.

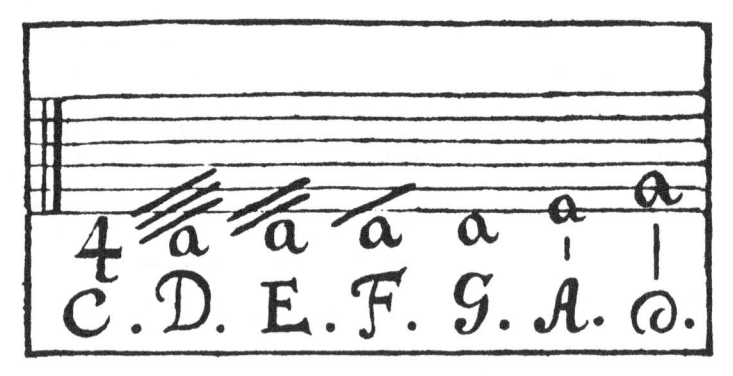

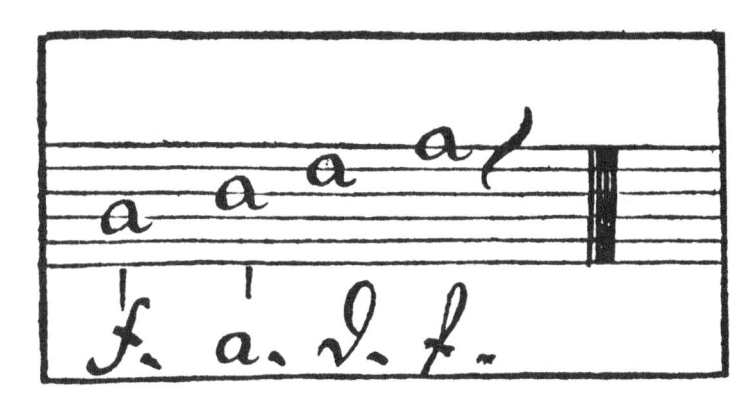

These must be compared and tuned in the following manner by unisons and octaves.

Although all courses on the lute are designated *a*, they are distinguished by lines and diagonal dashes so that they can be located easily. The open courses, which are all indicated with the *a*, are only struck with the right hand and not touched with the left. The following, however, are fingered directly behind the frets.

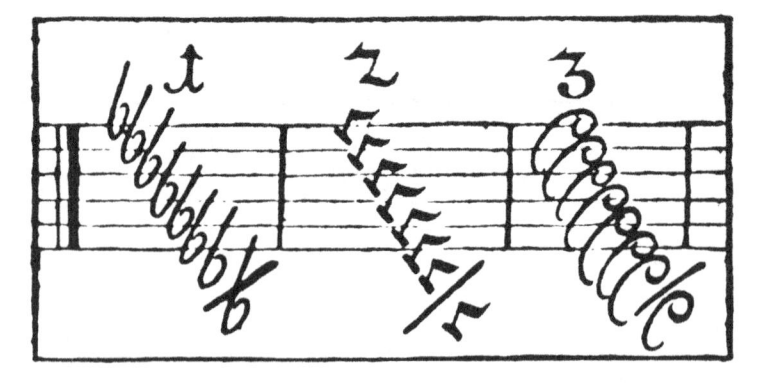

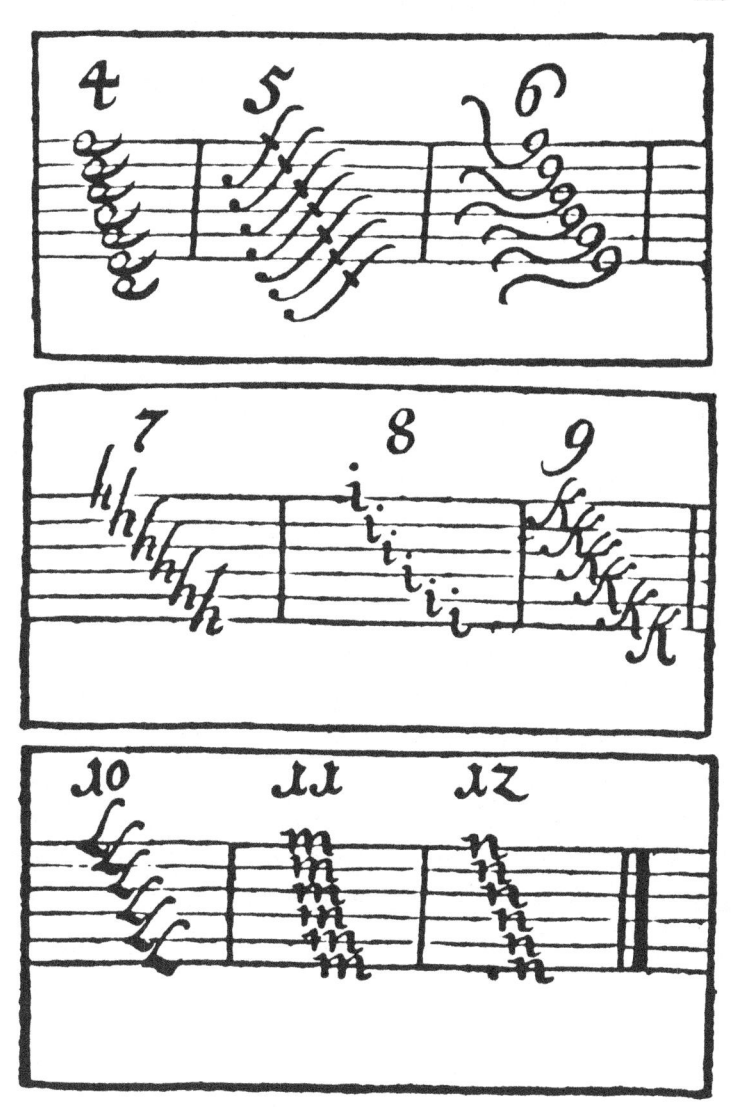

These are the frets that are distinguished by the other letters of the alphabet as shown. If the player wishes to find a letter from an intabulated piece, he needs only to see if it is on the first, second, or third line, and so forth, and then he finds the course. For example, if there is an **f** on the third line, it should be sought according to the alphabet on the third course, counting from the chanterelle. It is as if to say, all open strings are called *a*, the first fret on all strings is called *b*, the second *c*, the third *d*, the fourth *e*, the fifth *f*. When you have the fret where the intabulated letter lies, you can find it immediately.

If a beginner objects that the two thinnest courses are single and the others double, he should not trouble himself about it, since the double strings are tuned either in unison or in octaves. I have mentioned this objection because some people may think of such objections if they do not know the reason. I do not know if it should be called a flaw that the lute's positions are marked with bands of gut strings, as Herr Mattheson asserted on page 281 of his *Orchestre*. He talks about the violin and says that it is one of the most difficult instruments, because its positions are not marked with bands as on lutes, theorboes, and so forth. This learned remark stems perhaps from the fact that very few people have seen violins. Which instrument is the most difficult has not been determined, because anything can be made easy or difficult depending upon the capacity of people for it.

To avoid spending too much time with extraneous things, it will now be necessary to discuss fingerings. It is a science to use the fingers correctly, so that by their correct placement a flowing melody is promoted with more ease than would otherwise be the case. The fingerings can be conveniently categorized as easy, difficult, and uncommon. In the easy and common fingerings, attention must be paid to natural order, since it makes everything necessary for knowledge easy. When *b* appears on the first fret, it can be taken by no other finger than the first. With the other frets, the player must look at the preceding and following ones, thus I will here undertake to show the most necessary and prominent cases and indicate the fingers with numbers.

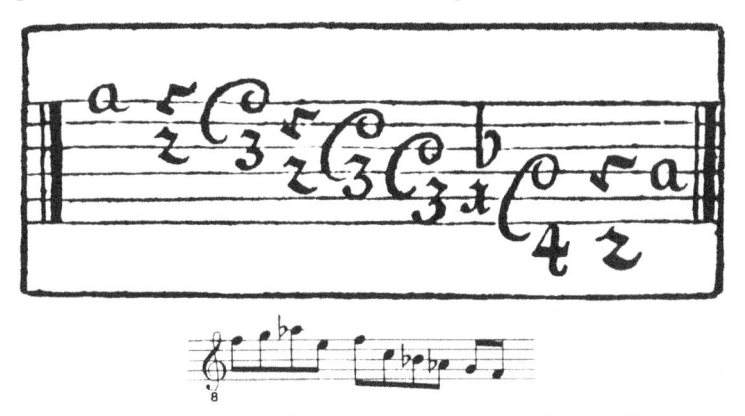

The third finger is seldom used, mostly only in full chords. The fourth is commonly used in cases where the first finger takes a letter, no matter which fret, and from there the melody falls on tones on the third fret. This must also be taken into account in reverse.

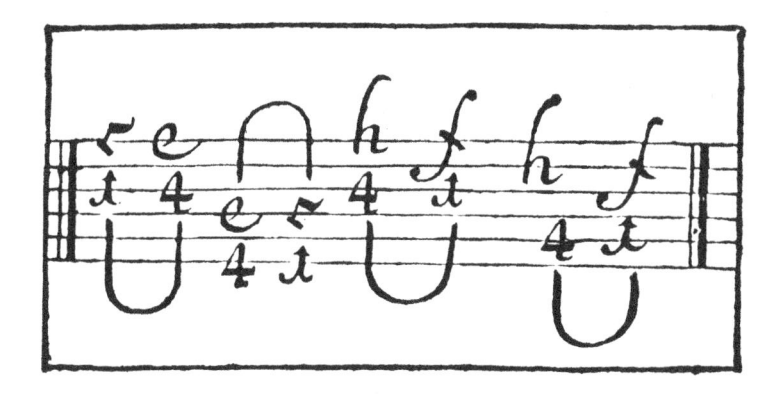

The lower arcs show the letters that differ by three frets from each other, and the reader will note that in, these cases a letter in alphabetical order, both forwards and backwards, has been omitted. Just as no rule is without an exception, the little finger must often be used on the farthest letters, so that the player can more easily follow with the others, which are closer to the other fingers.

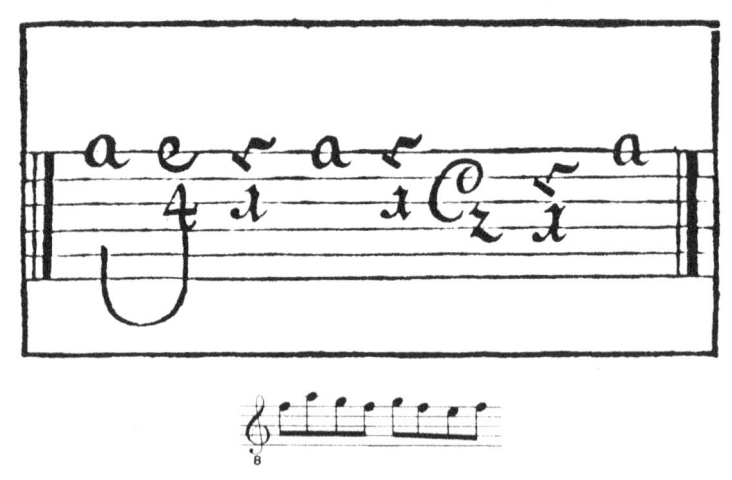

The second finger is mostly used when the first finger has taken a letter and the melody proceeds to the immediately following fret.

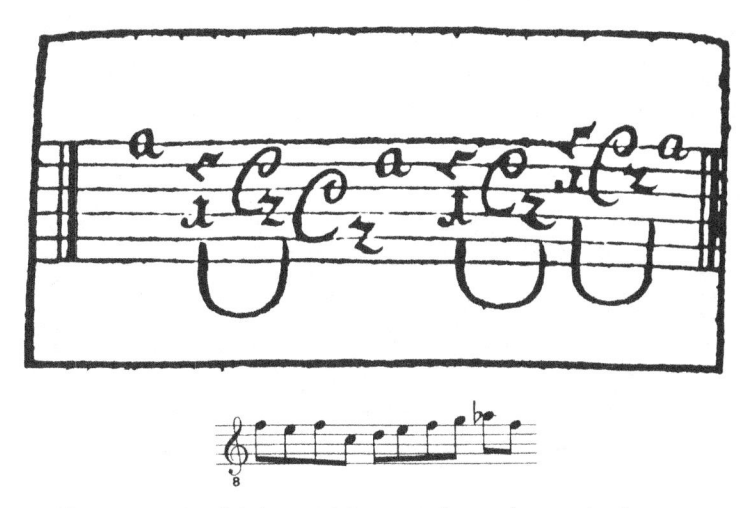

However, in high positions, when the melody moves back one fret from the letter taken by the little or fourth finger, the player has to employ the second finger.

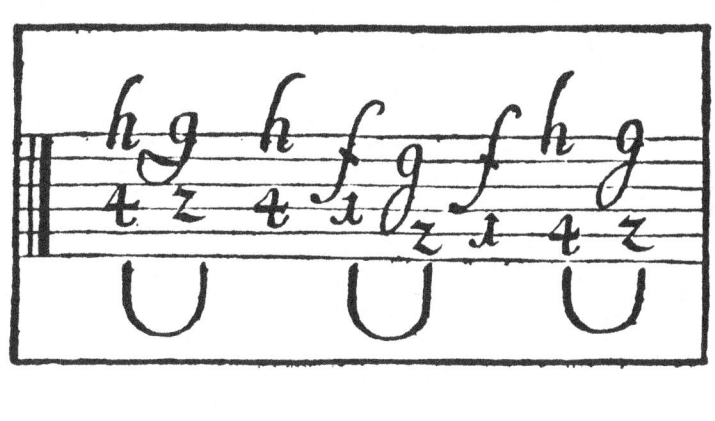

Rather often it happens that the player has to climb from the depths to the heights and from the heights into the depths (I have chosen these words for clarity), then the player must use one finger twice in a row.

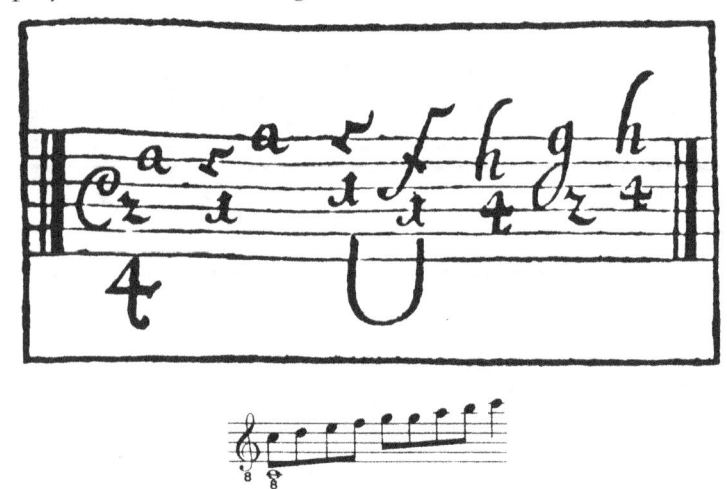

When the player must move the fingers from higher letters to lower ones, in reverse alphabetical order [the fingers go in reverse as well], so that no awkward leaps or crossovers result.

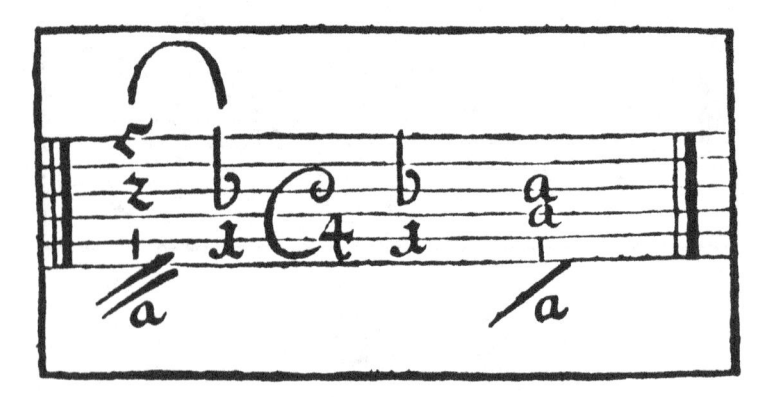

Difficult fingerings are not difficult when the player knows the advantages of them. One of these is the *barré*. Here it must be noted that the first finger is to be placed straight and unconstrained behind the fret, without special straining of the nerves, so that the fleshy part of the finger and the string fit close together. If the player allows the finger to bend or fails to lay it correctly across with a curved hand, the strings will not be pressed sufficiently onto the fingerboard and will buzz against the flesh of the fingers and not give the slightest pure tone. Most cases when the player must use the *barré* have been established. It occurs primarily when whole chords appear at one fret.

Sometimes other fingers aid in a *barré*.

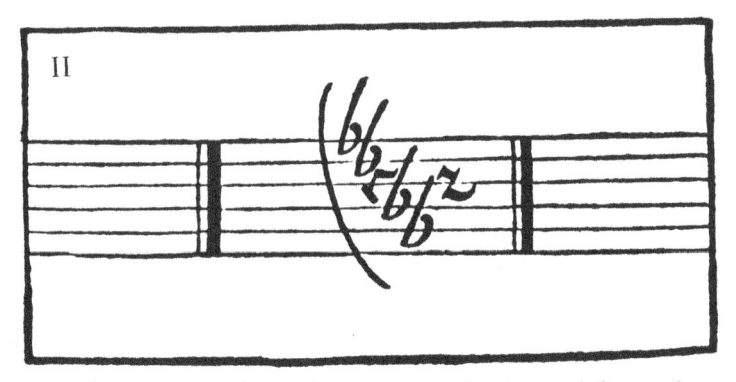

[Tablature example II]

It also occurs when I have to use the second finger for a bass.

[Tablature example III]

[Staff notation showing chords I, II, III]

The player also has to keep the *barré* and carry on with the other fingers, as in this example.

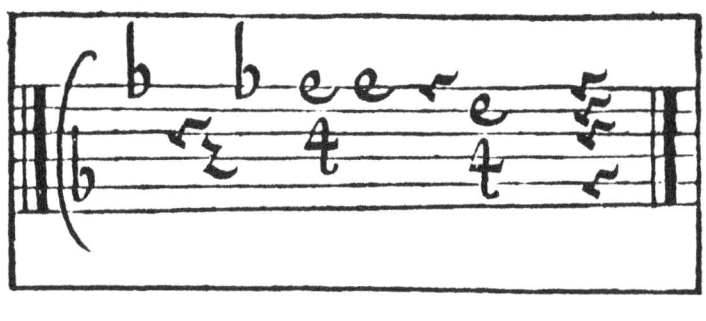

From time to time the player even uses two other fingers in full chords.

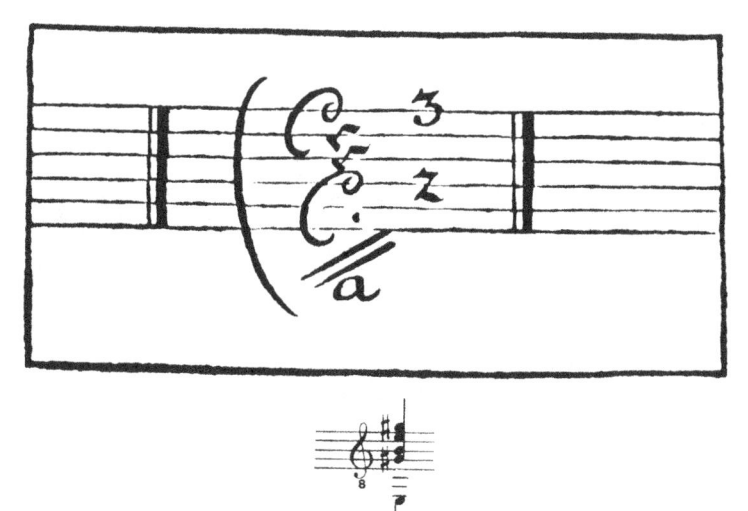

When two of the same letter appear on one fret, the player does not have to use a *barré*, but may use the third and fourth fingers.

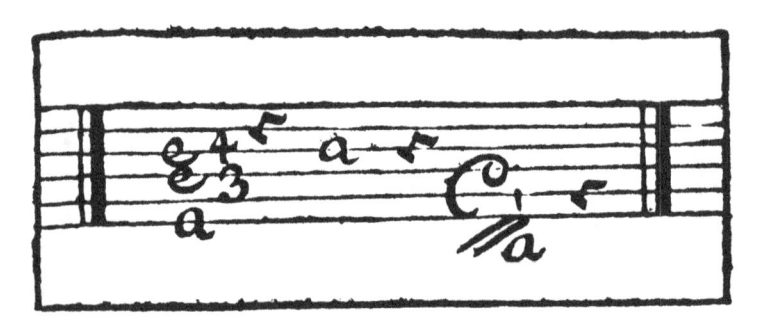

Yet frequently, when the little finger has to change strings in the high register and the letters stand somewhat apart, the player will bar strings with good effect.

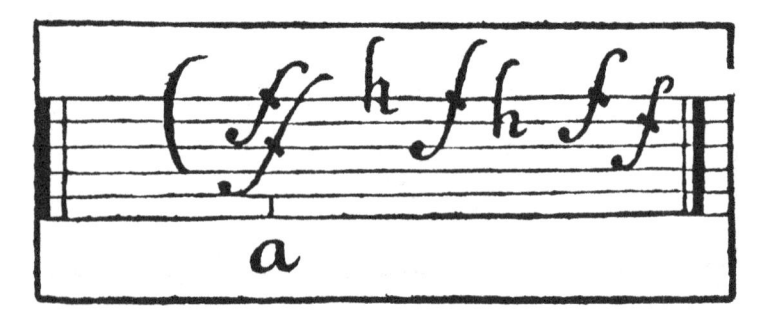

Much more fuss could be made about this matter, but I believe it unnecessary, since most amateurs can themselves judge what is comfortable and uncomfortable. No rule is so sacrosanct that it cannot admit of exceptions from time to time. Whereas I have previously talked about normal fingerings, we shall now turn to irregular ones, since crossing and sliding of fingers is sometimes necessary.

This example could, of course, be fingered otherwise, but it would not be so satisfactory, since it would only unsettle the whole position of the hand, especially at a quick tempo. The other passage where the slide appears is fingered in the following manner.

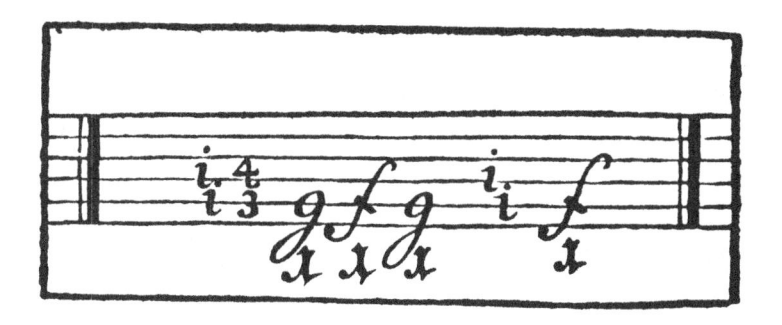

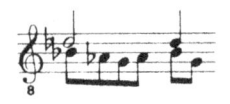

It is impossible to show here all fingerings and passages. Thus it is enough to know the main principles from which others can be derived according to the judgment of comfort.

Methods used by the old lutenists to promote dexterity of the hand are sometimes ridiculous, although some may still be suitable. In Italy, as Besard says, they put heavy leaden rings on their fingers to stretch them. They also made a kind of glove, perfumed with all sorts of stimulating things. Others stretched the fingers out on boards. Many made use of salt-tartar oil which, they maintained, stimulated the nerves when the hand was brushed with it. Some believed that the hands should be kept very clean by constant washing, for not only are the sinews and tendons stimulated, but also speed is promoted by the wetting of the hand.

For my part, I believe that one or the other method may well contribute to conserving the hand, but as for dexterity, it can only be acquired through moderate practice, so that the spirit is not fatigued but always remains alert. One or the other piece can also be taken and played until it is learned almost by heart. When this has been done often, the fingers cannot help but become as fast as the thoughts, for by such means the steadiness of the hand is greatly promoted.

No one should assume that I wish to introduce constant memorization, which I only ordain for the beginning, so that the player will not have to search too long in the future. The whole matter only applies in the beginning to a few pieces that the novice should take the trouble to study with appropriate constancy, for it will serve his hand well the rest of his life. It is also better to first study little with accuracy than much carelessly.

Everyone can have an instrument made for his hand. The size of the hand, and slender, thick, short, and small fingers do not affect it in the slightest, unless something is wrong with the hand.

The old lutenists transcribed much other music for the lute, for they made use of this means, as mentioned above, to accommodate their instrument to everything. But today, since it has a completely different reputation, transcription should take place only in thought, when someone has heard something pretty, and for this considerable practice is required. The lute is so rich in tone that we need nothing else, and we have many beautiful concerti, trios, and other music that sounds much less forced.

Among the old lutenists was a Frenchman, Antoine Francisque, born in Paris, the first to introduce transcription.[41] After him, others continued the accomplishment, namely Matthaeus Reymann in his *Psalmodiae [Davidis]* and *Floribus Musicae*[42], of which he wrote two books; Adrian Denss in his *Florilegium*; Joachim van den Hove (a man who was very famous in this field at his time); in his *Florida* and *Delitiae Musicae*; Joachim Georgius, [Georg] Leopold Fuhrmann, and [Elias] Mertel, who transcribed

---

41. In his *Le Trésor d'Orphee* (Paris, 1600), Francisque includes instructions on transcribing music for lute. However, even the first published book of lute tablature, Spinacino's *Intabulatura de Lauto* (Venice, 1507), contains transcriptions from vocal music, and the practice was common throughout the sixteenth century.
42. Reymann published a volume entitled *Noctes musicae* in Heidelberg in 1598 and his *Cythara sacra sive Psalmodiae Davidis* in Cologne in 1613. I have found no record of a *Floribus musicae*.

preludes and fantasias; [Emanuel] Adriansen in his *Pratum Musicum*; and [Jean Baptiste] Besard in his *Thesaurus Harmonicus*.

If there should be any contemporary lutenist who desires to transcribe this or that piece of today's music, he must understand music, lute fingering, and how the tablature letters correspond to musical tones. The diagram of the lute fingerboard in Part II, Chapter 1, will serve him well.

This is all I will write about fingerings and other principles. The rest, for which I cannot give rules, I will leave to the judgment of the reader, since many things can be better demonstrated privately than written. An amateur, however, needs conventional notation for no more than learning mensuration, because it consists of a certain proportion of time. He should accustom his imagination, through frequent practice, to be attentive to it, until he can be taught by a good master.

I have not wished to bind myself here to any metaphysical terminology, but rather have attempted to make everything as comprehensible as possible. If some other observations should occur to me, this book can be improved later, for Rome was not built in a day. I therefore trust that the judicious reader will in the meantime be content with these few.

CHAPTER IV

The Most Elegant Ornaments [Manieren] on the Lute, Their Designation, Nature, and What is Primarily Important Today

F the reader now has become thoroughly acquainted with everything pertaining to the fundamentals, then I will do well to mention the most elegant ornaments that occur on the lute and that are peculiar to it in their execution. Before I take this upon myself, it will be necessary to set down a general concept, so that the reader can see what their essence actually depends upon. This consists of a dexterity of the hand deliberated with reason, giving a tone its proper power through pressing or shaking, so that when the player ornaments the middle tones, some of which comprise the melody, the music may emerge freely and flowing in a singing manner. All instruments must imitate the well-cultivated human voice. For if a beginner on the lute, who does not yet have an idea of its characteristics, wished to play all the letters he sees and the tones hidden in them, the sound would emerge very crudely and roughly.

Since it is here primarily a question of imitation of the singing voice, I will mention the curious inspiration of the ancients who ascribed to birds, man's skill of the throat with which he expresses tones and projects to one distance or another. They stated that man had learned this distinction from the birds, as Lucretius,[bi] and Rheimann who concurred with him, assert. Man is the most perfect and rational creature and the most skilled of all animals at arts and sciences, the principles of which lie in his nature. Thus how could another creature have more perfect organs necessary for systematic song than man possesses? Those instruments played by bow strokes and the wind instruments are certainly the most adroit at imitating *cantabile,* because the player can draw and sustain a tone on them for a long time. However, those that must be sounded by a percussive stroke, such as the clavichord, harpsichord, and lute, can produce perfect *cantabile* as well as the others, except that the player cannot draw and hold a tone as long as he would like, for it still sounds after the stroke but soon dies away.

The slurring of tones, which is technically called the hammer stroke and pull-off (*Einfallen und Abziehen*) comes out very naturally and in a singing manner on the lute. The essence of a hammer stroke is to fall upon a tone that is still sounding with the second or fourth or little finger a second or third higher without striking the note with the right hand. The pull-off is the opposite; from higher, still-sounding tones the finger is pulled off to lower ones. Both ornaments are designated as shown.

The trill (*Trillo*) consists of a movement that is begun rather slowly and softly but is continued faster and stronger. Before making the trill, a higher tone must be played, according to whether the piece is in the major or minor mode, then the movement can be suitably made after the player has struck a tone. It is designated as shown.

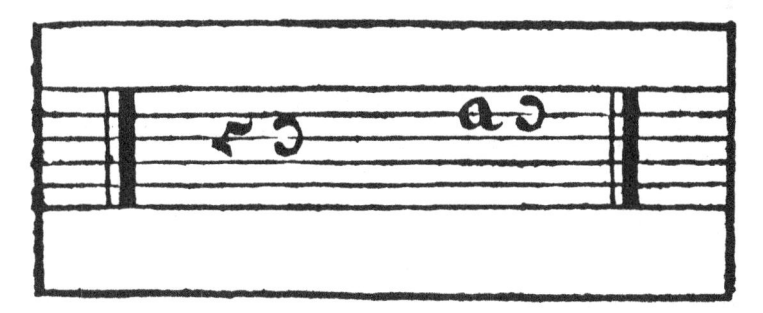

Vibratos or *Bebungen* are designated in two ways according to the context. Those high up on the neck are marked as shown. Their execution consists of firmly gripping the designated letter with the little finger, and when the string has been struck with the right hand, the left hand, continually pressing, is moved rather slowly now to the left, now to the right side. It must be noted that during the motion the thumb, which otherwise remains firmly in the middle of the neck, is let free and loose, for in its fixed position it would only hinder the motion. The essence and nature of the vibrato consists of a pleasant doubt or anticipation, begins to waver, and seems to the ear somewhat higher, then somewhat lower while still wavering.

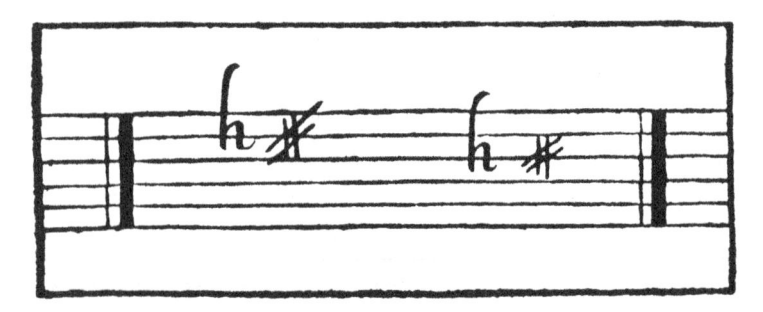

Those executed in the lower register have, to be sure, the same nature, but their method of production is completely different from the first kind. It consists of placing the appropriate finger down and pulling the string back and forth with it, so that the same kind of *Bebung*, or wavering tone, is produced.

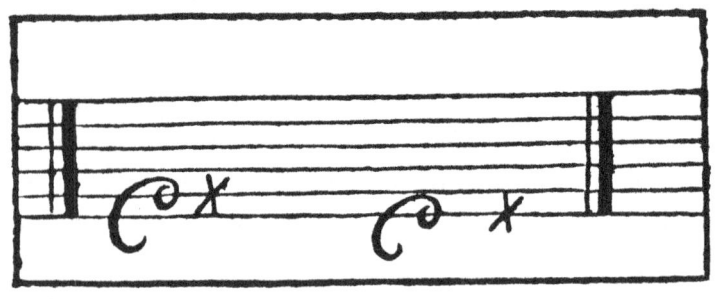

The reason that these vibratos are not made with an open hand as are the above is that there is not enough freedom to operate down next to the pegbox, because the hand, the closer it is to my body, not only requires more weight but also more force in gripping, so that the pulling motion was invented to aid it.

These are the ornaments that are primarily designated in lute tablatures for the beginners, until they learn to apply them at the appropriate places in unornamented pieces themselves. Yet one must not think that all of them are indicated there, because many cannot be indicated as well as invented and executed [extemporaneously]. The best ornaments depend upon the player's invention and the manner in which he produces them. He must alternately moderate or force the sound of his lute in such a way that it does not exceed the nature of the instrument—we cannot give strict rules for this. Each player must himself judge what sort of affect he wishes to express with this or that ornament.

A player must make a distinction between playing alone and in ensemble. If he plays alone, he can delay a bit longer and do more ornamentation, especially in slow pieces. However, it must not be excessive, for too many ornaments, particularly if not applied in the right places, garble the music and melody. In quicker pieces, the best *Manier* is nothing more than neatness and clarity, and if someone wanted to make many other additions it would be as ridiculous as chasing rabbits with snails and crabs.

If you play with others it is necessary to know beforehand what sort of method the other player has, so that you can adjust to it. For you have to imitate and defer to the other to a certain extent, and adopt the same method, for if diverse styles are used, not only the harmony but also gracefulness is ruined.

A run also belongs to musical grace and elegance, and it sounds very good when applied in slow pieces (airs, sarabandes, and so forth) and at cadences as the singers apply it. I mentioned above that now and then passing tones can well be applied between two notes, so for the sake of clarity I will here give an example.

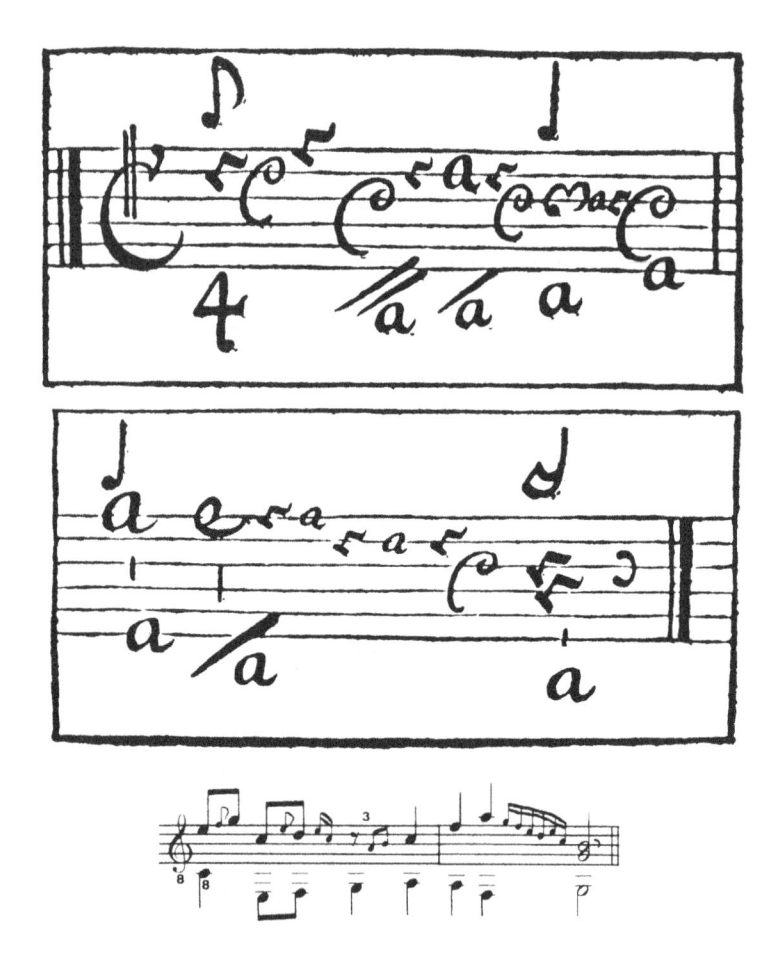

The small letters are the intermediate tones, the large ones comprise the main melody. If they are to be placed between the melody notes, they must not interfere with the tempo and the mensuration. Normally a run will progress either upwards or downwards.

However, there are so many that it is impossible to set them all down here. You must learn from good masters where they can be applied, for although this can be mentioned in general, it cannot be determined exactly. I merely wished to give a few here for the pleasure of beginners who do not understand much music, so that they would have some idea of it and be, better suited to the matter. An amateur who is attracted to the lute must not attempt to pick up everything at once, for as with other instruments, he must concern himself with strength or dexterity of the hand, and then elegance will gradually come of its own accord.

CHAPTER V

Playing With Proper Taste

ALL fine arts and sciences occasionally suffer the fate whereby an individual makes judgments about them exceeding his knowledge. Noble music, which has been cultivated more and more from its origin to our own time, has experienced this not only in ancient times but today as well. The many thousands of people in a country, not to mention in the world, will disagree about a subject of which not everyone understands the fundamentals, because everyone has an opinion according to insight and intelligence. A noble spirit that has the nature of the eagle need not pay attention to all this, but rather must ponder how to fly ever higher in his art. If he understands his music and instrument perfectly, he must only go passively and entice [the tones], to which Titius or Gavolenus had an inclination, then he will be able to adjust accordingly.

If we thoroughly investigated wherein the best taste is found, we could only say that it is "an understanding sharpened through much practice and experience in a given art, one with which a person can grasp all the contributing details without self-interest or prejudice and assess the quality of it according to the proportion of its value." This taste in the arts is only to be found among noble and cultivated minds. Thus a virtuoso will do well to demonstrate his art before these people with great industry and skill, for from such people he can expect not hollow praise but rather the truth about his playing.

Every nation has something special in its music, and it is best to assemble the particularly outstanding elements of each and apply them to one's own ends. A *galant* artist must not be narrow, but rather should be able to change himself like a chameleon. Merry Italy, which was, so to speak, destined by heaven to be the mother of all sorts of fine arts, has something "very melancholy, excellent, singing, serious, flowing, and ingenious in its music. A lively spirit or essence ordinarily accompanies its melodies. All manner of strange and peculiar passages make such a pleasant· impression upon the feelings that they are better heard than sufficiently described."[43] Their country is charming, thus most Italians are more intent upon sensuous things than rational matters.[bj]

Galant and complacent France, which commonly shows itself at its best on the strings, has a "free and lively nature and makes music more facetious, indifferent, and frivolous than all other civilized nations, thus it affects women more than serious and genuine temperaments."[43] However, since Lully came, they have applied *cantabile* more to solely instrumental pieces than vocal music. This is because their language does not admit as many vowels as Italian, in which we can do ornaments even on words that have no particular textual significance.

Whereas the Italian manner is grave and the French taste diverting, we in Germany have adopted both, since our nation loves change and jumps from one thing or extreme

---

43. Baron puts these passages in quotes but gives no source.

to another. To make this even clearer, it was recognized by an artful and virtuoso painter, who portrayed with extraordinary skill all other nations on a canvas according to their usual costumes. But when he came to the German, he left him standing stark naked like Adam in Paradise, and painted him a piece of cloth under his arm so that he could dress himself as he wished. Beyond this, the German thinks highly of physical exercise, follows the new fashions intently, and thinks he has done enough when he pays no attention to other *galant* things besides languages and what he learned in school, despite the fact that he could develop his taste much more.[bk]

Many Germans want to acquire all wisdom and skill from foreign countries and spend a great deal of money and trouble in the process. Very few notice what fine artists and people they have in their own fatherland. If we throw some light on this, we see that very few Germans are sophisticated or adroit, but most have a good taste for *Lacrymis Christi Vino Montepolziano, vin de Bourgogne,* and champagne that they have brought home to serve the fatherland.[bl] Now that we have seen in general what the taste of each nation consists of, every rational virtuoso will easily be able to perceive why it happens that his accomplishments are more praised than promoted, because many enormous sums of money are granted only to foreigners for their traditional bagatelles and not to natives.

Now if a virtuoso or lutenist (by which I mean those who have earnestly applied themselves to the instrument) has the honor of playing for someone who has heard a great deal and is a connoisseur, he must first distinguish himself with preludes, fantasias, fugues, and so forth, so that it can be seen that he is capable of thinking, and then he can undertake other good things. Because this sequence is preferred by the most *galant* German masters, and we should always argue empirically, it can incontestably be considered the most tasteful manner of playing.

The keyboard, and thus the insight into the wide field of music, must be acquired along with technical skill. These prerequisites teach a clever head to meditate and to judge harmony. Whoever can think methodically, clearly, and cleverly is truly learned, and this requires no special proof because it is inherently correct. Similarly, no one can pass for a true musician if he cannot immediately give principles and derive as many conclusions from them as he wishes. Who would wish to deny that harmony is the principle from which all manner of alterations and passages can be derived, which can well serve in preludes and fantasies? This can be seen in the following illustration.

148

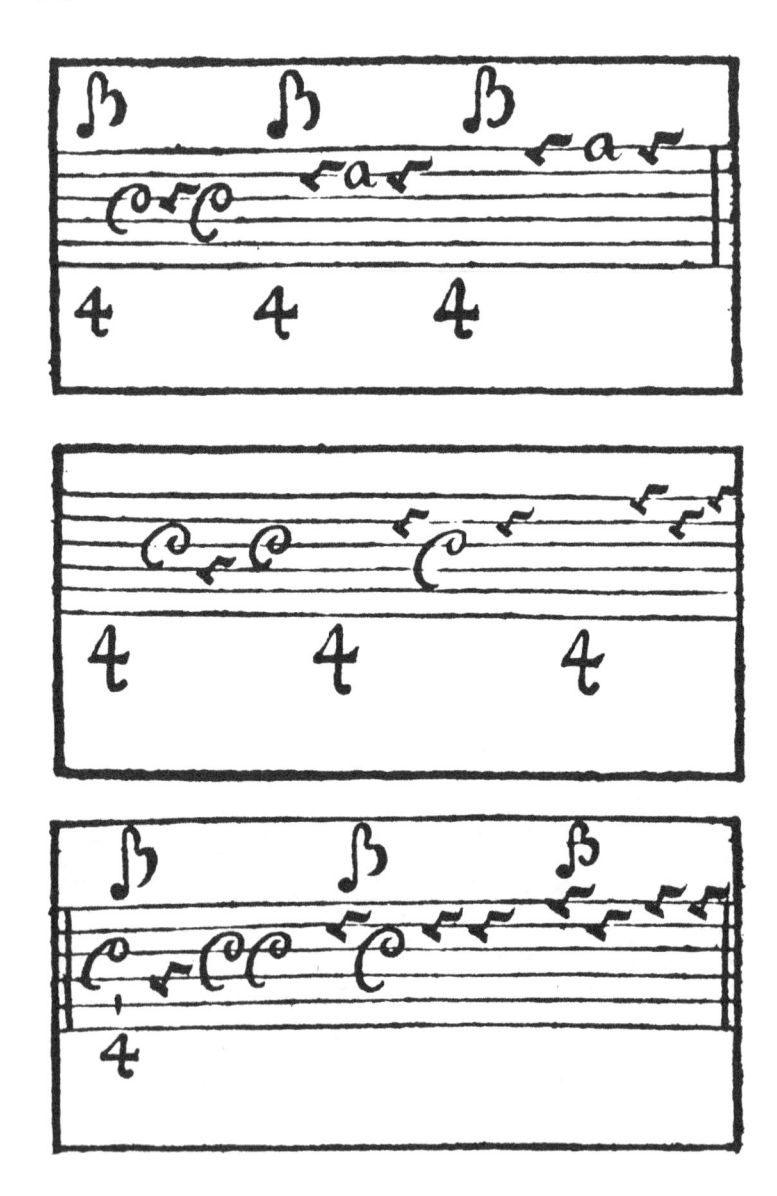

All of this flows out of a single chord, and such derivations could be extended much further, especially if we used the higher and lower registers. I have shown this here so that it can be seen how a single chord can spawn many passages. Now if you add an inventive genius who is more or less profound, then by much permutation and inversion of tones, a good and lovely prelude will necessarily result. Of course, I would not actually vary a single passage so much, for then the harmony would be all the same and it would be apparent that the performer had little genius and resolve.

The origin of the prelude can be nowhere but in the

church, since it was introduced for the purpose of giving the common people, who knew little about singing, a sense of the key of the hymn to follow, although they were sometimes extemporized on other occasions as well. Fantasias doubtless came from preludes, for after music became more *galant* they were retained so that the performer could show and exercise his imagination. Their essence consists of an unordered connection of many passages and thoughts that can be executed according to all kinds of mensurations and meters at will. It will of course do if such things are well composed on paper, but it is as if the spirit and the power are missing, so to speak, if they are not produced extemporaneously. For when the player is thinking and abstracting from other objects, as it were, and he pursues this or that invention with the agility of his mind, then it cannot exactly transpire that the imagination should be empty of other ideas that can contribute something to peace of mind. You must only notice when an excellent musician is not in good spirits, and you will see that his whole being is strained in the music, especially what he plays extemporaneously, and also that no such supply of ideas is present.

However, if you actually observe it, you will find that the fantasia has the same character as poetic furor, although there are now and then some who do not think much of it. Meanwhile, it is certain that occasionally a player is moved to express good inventions for which he would normally not have the force of spirit. To what should we attribute this? I am of the opinion that we must count this among the secret, hidden, and unexpected forces of nature, for she occasionally has the desire to create some extraordinary works.

Now I do not wish to consider what is required for a poet who wants to accomplish something that will earn him applause, for others have already done that. However, it is certain that you can sooner show a great number of learned people than one real poet or other excellent artist in music, although Mänling, in the preface to his poetic lexicon, maintains with grandiloquent words (but not with solid reasons) that such people can reach the peak of perfection through mere instruction. If we accept the latter idea as certain, then that which is born in musicians and poets would be of no further use, and it would naturally follow that everyone, without distinction, would attain the same perfection. Because we can easily see the fallacy of such an opinion, we will do well to respect those people whom God has given special and extraordinary gifts and to promote their welfare.

Now that we have considered the art of playing preludes and fantasias and whatever could be mentioned along with it, it will perhaps be well to observe and judge the art of regular pieces in the same meter. To this genus I count concerti, trios, and pieces of which several are placed one after another in one key and are called suites.

Concerning the concerti and trios that have the lute as their main voice, the allegro and presto, and so forth, must be composed rather long, but the adagio shorter, so that change is not stifled. When change occurs often, it is the true delight that we feel in music. The movements must be so constituted that the passages and phrases are thought out according to the lovely, *galant* music of today. Performers must take care that when other instruments accompany the lute they do not drown it out, but rather let it sound out above the others, since it is the principal instrument. This can be better accomplished if the other instruments cut their accompaniment short and do nothing beyond helping the lute stand out in concerted passages and supporting the gentle harmony. When the lute is supposed to stand out, it is poor taste to make many ornaments and *Kribuskrabus*, so to speak, with the accompaniment, since here the greatest elegance consists of simple clarity and accuracy.

Suites must, of course, have *galant* ideas according to new music, but should be executed with moderation because they are played solo, where the player considers forte and piano both in the right-hand touch and in the motion of the left. For because such pieces are produced to please, and because pleasure comes from frequent change, a master as well as an amateur must follow custom, since the piece belongs not to him alone but to others as well.

Previously we have spoken solely of taste in general, but now it is time to consider the absurd and corrupt taste of some masters and audiences. Some masters love to hear themselves in public, and sometimes when they get up a full head of steam they cannot stop. Then the audience will, of course, grow weary, no matter how lovely and admirable it be. For just as taste in general cannot always take the same food, the ear cannot take much of the same melody. We must practice due moderation in all things, so that it does not appear that a player is attempting to force someone to admire his playing. Thus everything that can be called short and sweet is to be sought after, so that those who hear it have a desire to hear more in the future.

Now those who occasionally have the opportunity to hear highly skilled masters can often not tame their tongues, either out of pleasure or ignorance, and they chat and discuss as though they had lost all their five senses. They are so brazen that they disturb the attention of others, and it is not unjust to compare them to irrational animals that cannot make use of pearls or other valuable things. Such people have, as Gracián says, a lamed soul, and are better off among their own kind than in circles where things proceed in an orderly and rational manner.

Some others only admire what assaults the senses with a loud noise. These people belong more in village taverns and bars than in places where everything is beyond their horizon. However, some who are of a thoughtful disposition wish to know of nothing but gentleness and prefer a pensive nature above all other beauties. These people have taste, to an extent, but because it is for a matter that essentially does not do much, it is similarly to be rejected.

All things must be proportionate, as circumstances permit, and nothing must be too much or too little, for this subject will otherwise please only one person rather than many—the aim to which music must certainly be directed. Those people who in the above-mentioned circumstances cannot accustom themselves to reason and moderation are to be considered almost like barbarians, to whom everything is the same if they only howl and hear lots of noise[bm]—although Petits de la Croix makes much ado about a Persian composer Abdel-moumen [Safí al-Dín, 'Abd al-Mu'min] and considers that he was the Lully of his day.[bn]

We shall leave such ridiculous people to their tastes and think, as Aristophanes did, that someone who can perceive delicacy and wonderful harmony in a reasonable manner and make use of it for himself is a wise, clever man furnished with all conceivable perfections. On the other hand, we should consider a man who has no rational taste either one who has lost his senses or one in whom the life spirits are antagonistic to each other in their actions.[bo]

There needs to be no more praise here, since what is important is not words but the subject itself. I wished to do no more here than to distinguish the true from the false and the good from the bad, because everyone will see for himself which kind applies to him.

CHAPTER VI

Thoroughbass

WHOEVER wishes to excel on the lute must earnestly apply himself to the study of everything necessary for artistic perfection, so that when it is now and then needed, he will not be deficient in things that could show him off to the best advantage.

To these things belongs first of all thoroughbass (*General-Bass*), which is called *generalis* because it includes all of the harmony for a given piece in the numbers above the notes. Praetorius tells us why it was invented, referring to an old author, Agostino Agazzari, whose reasons are primarily the following three:

1. Because of today's practice and style in singing, since we compose and sing just as if we were reciting an oration.
2. Because of convenience.
3. Because of the great amount, variety, and multitude of works and parts that are necessary for the music.

It is not indicated exactly when thoroughbass was first played on the lute, but it is nonetheless certain that it was practiced on the lute long before a hundred and seven years ago. Although Herr Mattheson attributes the invention of thoroughbass solely to later times, placing the date around the year 1600, this is written only on his authority and is far from proven. He names an Italian, Ludovico Viadana, as the inventor of it and says that he wrote the first treatise on this material, but it could be that with considerable insight and method Viadana made a systematic science out of what he found in a rather crude state.[bp]

Because mere historical knowledge alone will not suffice for us without knowing some means of comfortably attaining it, I will take the liberty of discussing it a bit, as far as the subject will suffer it. Now Praetorius, in his above-mentioned treatise, touched upon this and that in this doctrine, but did no more than say how a player should conduct himself in accompaniment, so that this was then only for those people who were already fairly perfect and skilled; however, he did give them some directions concerning elegance. Monsieur Franz le Sage de Richée long ago promised a treatise on how to learn thoroughbass on the lute, but to my knowledge he has not kept the promise.

On this subject we can do no more than propose ways and means to attain this noble and splendid goal. Therefore one must first have a sound foundation in music and keyboard before undertaking to study the lute. For thereby the novice learns to distinguish octaves, thirds, fifths, sevenths, and so forth, and to know how all other pertinent, signs should be employed in harmony. If he is now sure of such things, he should acquaint himself with the lute fingerboard pictured in Part II, Chapter I [page 99], together with all the courses and the musical tones they produce, so that he will learn where the octaves and unisons are located; this knowledge will serve him to be able to methodically reach those chords and numbers that appear over the bass notes without excessive leaps. For just as it is allowed neither on the organ nor the harpsichord to abandon contrary motion, it is also a great error on the lute to search up and down the fingerboard for an unconstrained melody that can be had [without moving the hand]. Therefore it is advisable to acquaint oneself beforehand on the keyboard with *motus rectus et contrarius* and *transitus regularis et irregularis*,[44] and one will advance much faster in one's studies.

I do not see that it is necessary to explain these technical terms, since it cannot be done as clearly as on the keyboard. In addition, all those who have written about thoroughbass have elucidated it to such an extent that no further explanation is necessary here, since this subject requires people who have already acquired considerable musical knowledge. To more quickly attack the matter, it will be helpful to know the middle and doubling voices with every figure or chord, so that it is not necessary to ponder when looking at the notes and to bite one's nails over the figures.

The famous and learned *Kapellmeister* Heinichen in Dresden has made an effort to teach thoroughbass. He was so successful in his compendious method that it was received with great applause; the whole treatise on thoroughbass is to be highly recommended because it is written the most plainly, clearly, and completely of all. Therefore, for the sake of beloved brevity, I will here include a compendious table of every figure, middle, and doubling voice. It is excerpted from his book and included here because of its special use and value, and because not everyone possesses the book.

---

44. Parallel and contrary motion; passing tones on strong and weak beats.

Signaturen.	6	43	76	7	98	9	6 5	65 43	♭7		4 3	4♯	5♭
Mittel-Stimmen.	3	5	3	3	3	3	3	8	3		6	2	3
Verstärck. Stimmen.	8	8	8	5	5	5	··	··	5	5♭	··	6	6

                                        2   1

To be sure, some wish to learn thoroughbass on the lute without all the means proposed here, and they employ much more roundabout methods to achieve perfection. For a long time they set the regular thoroughbass triads in lute tablature and test what they have retained through this transformation and what is now missing. If they cannot make good progress, they seek refuge in the intabulation until the whole solo with its figures and mensuration bears fruit. They practice this in all keys until they finally, in one or two years, become rather skilled and can play a piece at sight if it is not extraordinarily difficult.

Such a method will of course do, especially if there is someone at hand to show them how to comfortably realize the figures until they get a certain ability. Be that as it may, I nevertheless recommend adhering to my first proposals, for they lead to a far greater understanding than the latter and not only bring the player to practical application but also give an enormous amount of guidance that contributes sense to the matter. In the meantime, the first instructions are for someone who in time will become a master, and the second for an amateur who has no desire to make it a profession, but only wishes to apply all that is said here to his own amusement.

What has been said above about the means of attaining ability in thoroughbass is of course sufficient to more or less introduce this subject, but because the lute is an instrument that cannot sustain a tone as long as the organ can, the gentle reader will not take it amiss if we here mention something pertaining to clarity. When a whole note appears in the bass with several figures above it, the player can, without disturbing the harmony, strike the bass with each figure and make four quarter notes out of a whole note.

This can also be done with half notes. If nothing but eighth notes appear in a measure, the chord can be struck over every second note, unless it is marked with a [different] figure.

Where suspensions appear, the note upon which the resolution occurs can also be divided.

Triple meters are special, in that the bass is struck with its chord and then the chord is repeated without the bass, but with the precaution that they are normal (*ordinaire*) chords and no further figures are indicated.

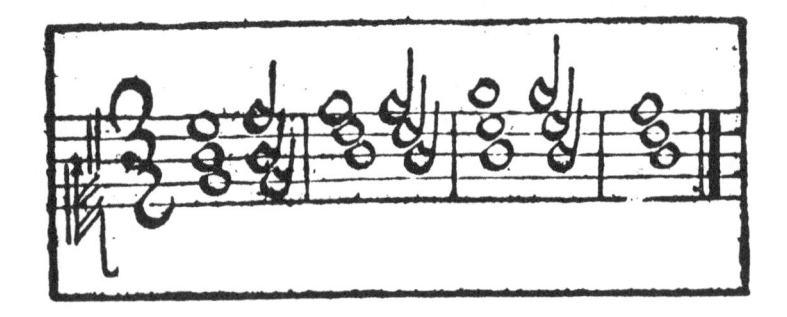

The reason for such rules is the strengthening of the harmony, which is necessary on stringed instruments like the lute that cannot make a long booming noise, because clarity is thus considerably promoted.

Before I resolve to close, it is necessary to consider how someone who desires to devote himself to thoroughbass should conduct himself while accompanying a singer or skilled instrumentalists. To play a praiseworthy accompaniment, a lutenist must always exercise judgment, defer, and refrain from all ornaments and arpeggios that he would apply ordinarily at other times; and when the singer or instrumentalist wishes to make a special expression, the accompanist should moderate his instrument so that he does not intrude upon the upper voice.

In such cases an accompanying instrument has no other function than to carry the upper voice and to help it along with its complete harmony, so to speak, as Praetorius recognized on page 145 [of his *Syntagma Musicum,* Vol. III]. Finally, the accompanist is required to pay close attention to the cadences and to delay a little when one comes in order to hear if the singer or instrumentalist perhaps wishes to make a *passaggio.* In these cases one must listen carefully so as not to enter too quickly or too slowly; then the accompaniment will have a good effect.

The many details that I have included here are for the benefit of those who desire to take up this discipline, so that before they proceed to it they will have a foretaste. A perfect musician who is resourceful in many other things will use his judgment more than all rules anyway. It would be almost impossible to include all details of such an important subject that demands so much, and there would have to be a special treatise written on it. Most of it depends upon actual practice, with which all theory must be secured and which I heartily recommend to everyone who desires to learn.

This is all that has occurred to me for the present about this special, ingenious, and beautiful instrument. I ask no more than that the gentle reader and all worthy and rational amateurs will be content for now with this, my good intention. If more that is necessary for the cultivation of this instrument should come to mind, I will not refrain from continuing the subject in an appropriate form.

But for now I shall bring my work to a happy

END.

SHORT APPENDIX OR DISCOURSE ON THE PROPENSITY FOR MUSIC, VIRTUOSI, AND ALL SORTS OF PREJUDICES

To praise something that requires no praise would be as ludicrous as attempting to make the sun's brilliance brighter with lights and torches. Noble music is in itself already something splendid, so that it would be fruitless labor to paint it a special repute with many pigments and colors. The singular esteem that it has enjoyed from the beginning of the world will not only protect its writings from mold and decay, but also its essence from all enemies until the end of the world. It will not be necessary here to discuss the wild Antheaeus, a Scythian king, who favored the whinnying of his horses above all music. The swinish Cynical philosophers may nonetheless say: *Magnæ reguntur urbes nam prudentia/At una cantu non queat regi domus.*[45]

Vockerod may write a thousand proclamations dishonoring this noble art and others may write thousands as well, but for my part, I do not mind if every fool wears his dunce cap. To all these numskulls and blockheads we can only counter with the dictum of the excellent Taubmann: *Quem non viva suo delectat musica flexu/Hunc ego non hilum cordis habere puto.*[46]

---

45. Great cities are governed with prudence, but one home cannot be ruled by a song.
46. "Whomever lively music does not delight in its melodiousness/has, I think, no heart at all."

All of learning has previously suffered the fate whereby there has sometimes come a period in which not only the nobility but even the clergy paid little attention to learning.[bq] I will not ask whether it is respectable for generous temperaments, because not only Kaiser Ferdinand III but also Kaiser Leopold I excelled the most glorious memories in their patronage. What King Louis XIII of France composed was included with special veneration by the famous Pater Kircher in his *Musurgia [universalis]* on page 690. Yes, today even the greatest princes and lords are not afraid to amuse themselves with musical instruments together with their virtuosi and to lighten the heavy burden of government with a draft of excellent harmony. Therefore this noble art is to be considered milk for the soul, a salve for affliction, a consolation in labor, and a medicine to dispel the hardships by which human life is surrounded.[br]

I will disregard what Athenaeus, Macrobius, Chassenaeus, Philippus Camerarius, Baldassar Castilionius, Robertus Valturius, and many others wrote about music's uses and excellence and will turn to the question of whether or not a man who feels an extraordinary propensity for this noble science is bound by the law of nature to pursue it. In addition, I will concern myself with examining the various types of virtuosi and the biases they hold about themselves and that others hold about them. Now there is certainly something to the fact that some do not wish to consider duty toward oneself as a duty extending to the talion, but only allege that duty toward others is the true object of natural law. When this happens, they think it only indirect, because *jus* and *obligatio* (the right and the obligation) would not be found in one and the same person.

I shall not pay any attention to that, but will simply reply that no man is capable of serving society energetically and giving satisfaction to natural law if he has not recognized his propensities, whereby his skill may contribute something to the advantage and pleasure of society. Therefore one is here chiefly compelled to closely observe wherein God as the Creator of all things has revealed his will, which is particularly in the moral nature of man. Reason and will, especially when they are directed at something good, give the best proof of divine providence and decree. Who does not know the manifold inclinations and the manifold opinions in which we can plainly see the many grades or levels of our reason and will and recognize the will of God as the greatest and noblest law of natural justice?

Now because it happens that every man commonly has the most inclination to a thing through which he can be of service and welcome to human society, he is also bound to cultivate it so that he may come closer and closer to the goal that the highest God intends, namely to live in society not like an animal, but rather usefully and innocently. Yet because temporal bliss rests primarily in this sort of life, it necessarily follows from the disposition of the Divinity that we should not only pursue necessary studies, but also those that are useful, acceptable, and awaken pure pleasure. Since man's moral nature is suited to such things, we can more certainly draw the conclusion that those talents mentioned in the Holy Scriptures are to be seen as none other than the capability whereby a man is suited to a field of study or profession, and this capability is called a gift, talent, or calling.

As previously mentioned, since the will of the Highest extends into human nature, it can be seen as nothing but a law—one that prescribes out of the light of nature what man should do and say. This doing and saying is proper when it promotes the happiness of mankind, but it requires recognition of that law and its motivation in everyone's conscience. Thus it necessarily follows that both *jus* and *obligatio* can occur in one person, although otherwise we count law a statutory obligation, but to the person, although this civil court is something quite different, because the law, cognition, and conscience are already implanted in human nature. Since man must be observed before he can be a worthy member of society, it follows that duty toward oneself could not be considered an indirect obligation, but rather, by the voluntary reason of God, as a direct one, and the consequences would follow immediately and directly.

There are thousands of examples of the unhappiness and ruin that compulsion has caused, therefore everyone is obliged to follow his imagination insofar as it motivates him to something good. Now if someone has a special penchant or entrusted talent for noble music (or to other fine studies), he is thus committed to make the most of it and acquire more, or to promote his innate character, because thereby natural law reigns. Even if he desired to deviate from it, he would not succeed so well in other things, nor could he be of as much use.

Those who from childhood have been driven by their moral nature to learn music, and who by virtue of their innate obligation and inner drive have cultivated it to a high degree, are called virtuosi by the contemporary and *galant* world. Their doings deserve more precise examination the more that prejudices are held against them. Even Diogenes Laertius gives cause for it when he says that he wonders how the musicians can tune their strings so purely and accurately and still have such ill-tuned manners.[bs] It is not necessary here to make much ado about the word *virtuoso*, because others have shown how broadly it is understood. Here it means a person who applies himself professionally to music and has made in it a sufficient study that he can excel many or even all others in his art.

The thought of Diogenes on musicians in general compels me to differentiate the goats from the sheep. In short, we can suitably separate them into rational and irrational ones, or even into useless ones. The first sort requires persons who are capable of making their fortune at noble courts, for here no simpletons or dunces will do. Rather such persons are required who not only have good conduct, but also possess reason, civility, and prudence in addition to the art in which they excel. Therefore it is incumbent upon each to also qualify himself in other useful things, so that everyone will have high esteem for him quite apart from the beauty, art, and entertainment he provides. For true honor consists in giving everyone a good conception and opinion of oneself and in using such means as promote this noble end.

However, some are so irrational as to assume that their art is alone sufficient to cloak all their vices and ill behavior, and they often commit the most scandalous and revolting excesses, notwithstanding their beautiful gifts and knowledge. The epigram of Diogenes applies solely to these people, for in their art they are virtuosi but in their behavior *vitiosi* (creatures of vice). It would lead us too far afield to talk about the jealousy, malevolence, and other unpleasant doings of the Messrs. Artists, and I would have to compose a special treatise about them, as Spizelius did with his *De vitiis literatorum*.

Now, whereas obstinacy is commonly ascribed to Messrs. Virtuosi as a great flaw, it will not be unsuitable to consider this or that aspect of it and to investigate where this prejudice might have its origin. Everyone knows well enough that there are greater numbers of inept, foolish, and thankless people in the world than prudent and clever ones. It is a special gift of God to be able to assess all things according to their value, and often in such matters an ounce of horse sense is worth more than ten pounds of instruction. Because a virtuoso musician will fare badly with such minds, he would do well to remember that it is better for a single wise man to recognize his merit than to be honored with tasteless and inappropriate eulogies by twenty others who do not comprehend the subject.

There are even some (which is very curious) who now and then like something, although they have not the slightest comprehension or taste for it. At this juncture an anecdote occurs to me, which because of its special nature I cannot leave untold. In Pluvicastro there was once a wealthy and handsome man who had a wedding. Because he was in need of music, which commonly enlivens joyous occasions, he sent for some musicians from the city and arranged for them to serve him with their harmony on his wedding day. When, in addition to other music, these musicians played a sonata that contained a fugue, he interrupted them in the middle of it, called to them with a fixed gaze, and said that he would take this prank that they had played upon him on his wedding day to the sagacious magistrat. The musicians, who suspected nothing ill of him, ascribed the bridegroom's hard words to drink, knowing that no one had done anything contrary to his duty.

However, when the wedding was over, Ignorantius (this was the handsome man's name) proceeded to the town hall and brought hard accusations against the musicians. Whether the accusations were civil or criminal is another matter. As soon as this action of libel (as I assume it was) was brought, the musicians, as is usual, were summoned. But when they were questioned and no more was found than that during the fugue Ignorantius had broken out in the above words, and that they did not know what had moved him to it, he explained quite pathetically that because they had played a trick on him by starting one after the other, whereas normally a piece should be played together, this did not please his ears and the musicians were liable.

They replied, however, that it was not their fault, because the composer had written it that way, and they had executed the piece as its nature demanded, and that this kind of music was called a fugue. Fortunately, some of the magisterial authorities had learned to play the harpsichord and knew that this type of piece was something very artful, and they helped awaken Ignorantius from his dream. After these proceedings, the musicians were asked to withdraw so that the suit might be carefully examined. They anxiously awaited what might happen, but instead of a sentence there followed general laughter, and thus the whole suit had the desired end.

Although this kind of story does not concern virtuosi, it is nonetheless true that many of us also meet such ignoramuses, and although they do not file suit, they have the same amount of reason as the above-mentioned saint. Because the most curious circumstances can arise, and most people expect more of a virtuoso than they are willing to reciprocally grant him, an intelligent virtuoso will do well to remember that "everything excellent is despised when it is used too much" (Gracián, Maxim LXXXV), and that "he who behaves commonly shows his bad temperament and low intelligence" (Gracián, Maxim CXVII). As long as arts and sciences have existed in the world, they have always suffered when the artists have known how to rationally preserve neither their own honor nor that of art. The good sense that a virtuoso observes before he plays for someone earns him a good name among intelligent people, since he will only display his art for those who know how to appreciate it. For it is better that he be commended by one wise man than praised by ten idiots who have no idea what is transpiring.

Therefore, we can draw the conclusion that a virtuoso must think well of himself, "for thereby he creates the presumption that a good name always has virtue as its foundation" (Gracián, Maxim X). The great teacher of politics and history agrees completely when he [Tacitus] says in *The Annals* IV: "*Contemtu famae contemni virtutes.*"[47] Thus not everything behind which often the greatest rationale is concealed is to be seen as caprice , and frequently a virtuoso can distinguish circumstances better than those for whom he plays.

The best method for preserving his reputation is not to show everything at once (Maxim XCV). Rarity is the mother of amazement, and Gracián is exactly right when he says that "One must always save something for tomorrow"

---

47. "By the condemnation of reputation, they are condemners of the virtuous."

(Maxim XVIII), for the reason that "custom dispels amazement" (Maxim CCLXXVII). Here we must proceed carefully, as with a palatable medicine, because excessive use can be harmful. Even a virtuoso loses all interest when he has to exert his life spirits too often in the face of boredom, particularly with things that demand quick resolve and meditation. The soul also needs its peace, as does the body, and it can become very fatigued through its own actions. For when the life spirits concentrate on one object, they forget, so to speak, their natural functions, and thus nothing more than satiety can result. From this, those who believe that amusing and pleasant studies can never become wearisome and disgust the person who pursues them will clearly see how necessary it is to establish the contrary. The sweetest sugar becomes bitter slime and gall, the most pleasant spices are turned into wormwood when they are excessively used, and they serve more to ruin the body than to stimulate it.

From all this it becomes quite apparent how unjust it is to accuse the excellent masters in music of any obstinacy when they cannot by these or those attendant circumstances give satisfaction to everyone's caprice, particularly when it can quite reasonably be said of most circumstances: *Malo modico civilque cultu contentum vivere, quam bona animi turoi quaestu pessimo exemplo foedare.*[48]

Since we have considered one or two kinds of virtuosi, it will not be inappropriate to observe the last kind, namely the useless ones, and to regard the above-mentioned opinion of Diogenes as a truth. The name "useless virtuoso"

---

48. I would rather live contentedly with a moderate and decent style of living than to sully the good things of the spirit with base grasping.

already sounds so dangerous that a person will lose his sight and hearing just to hear it, to say nothing of when he sees such a miserable thing. Those to whom God has given gifts with which to make themselves happy, but whom the singular and bizarre behavior of their unbearable genius makes unpopular with everybody, are more to be pitied than laughed at, although Gracián expressly says in Maxim CCXXIII that these eccentrics are only laughed at. Such a person has the misfortune of presenting himself in a bad light to everyone, although it is often not his intention. For when such a man is not granted many amenities by nature and does not enlighten and guide himself with reason and will, then the situation is certainly very bad.

To not linger too long in preludes, I will describe just such a useless and obscure virtuoso that I have known. This man is of moderate stature, lean, and has a longish, gaunt face, so that we can perceive more jealousy and malevolence than cheerfulness in his eyes, which are black but nonetheless without fire. When imagined misfortunes occur, he is so downcast and downright base that it is beyond description, and he despairs of almost any help, even when many means to this end appear. But when in his opinion something goes well, he is so arrogant and insolent that he would not care if he displeased everyone. Because he has nothing but false conceptions of all people, and sees them more as enemies than friends, one must tread lightly with him to avoid rocking the boat. In spite of all this, it is difficult not to inadvertently make him angry with a single look that he might have wished otherwise.

He is so presumptuous about himself that in spite of his small knowledge he considers himself far more intelligent than others, and he cannot bear it when someone remonstrates against him, even if he has asserted a great absurdity. He disputes in all disciplines and understands none of them. If he is in society, be it ever so *galant,* he is quite capable of disturbing the pleasure of the whole company with his tasteless conduct, for as Gracián says: "He wishes to censure others with his behavior." He is not able to keep a friendship, which is the true bond of human society, and if he does make friends it is usually with people of low and inferior station, because it flatters his pride to shine forth before them like a torch among tallow lamps and to be praised by them. He is otherwise very generous, so much so that he offers people his generosity even when he himself has nothing and is in need, but this does not come from a noble soul. In his preconceived opinions he shows such obstinacy that he would sooner endure the greatest misery than to consider abandoning them, even if he could change his position without others noticing.

Although this useless master has no merits in other matters, one has to praise him for one thing, namely that he plays his instrument quite gracefully and well, yet with such timidity that he imagines that all who listen to him are of his profession and understand the instrument far better than he. That makes him subject to failure at any moment, at a point when it seems that it should go very well, and for great fear and trembling he can be incapable of playing the simplest minuet.

These and other faults can still be corrected if only one's reason is adept at perceiving the difference between oneself and other people. For his own betterment a man must always keep excellent examples before himself and regard it as an honor and pleasure to associate with people who are more refined and clever than he, since he can profit greatly by such association. It is also desirable to strive, in as many situations as possible, to equal them in good manners. An intelligent, mature person must always become acquainted with his own strengths and weaknesses, so that he may accommodate himself to what will harm or be of advantage to him. All this a person can gradually learn if he pays constant attention to himself and never places too much confidence in himself, but rather remembers that others can accomplish something good as well. Our life is a precious good that has only been loaned to us by God, so that we may be better witnesses of his omnipotence and glory. Thus man cannot deprive himself of it, either through moping or by other means that only make life harder and more unpleasant, without thereby giving offense to the proprietor.

The opinion of Diogenes can be best applied to this type of mind, when it has been sufficiently examined. It is quite true that persons of this type can sooner change the tones of their instrument than their behavior; particularly, as in the present example, one who does not realize that his faults will grow more and more and finally become so firmly ingrained that he can no longer be polished, although from time to time he might feel the desire, like a peasant, for bloodletting. No man is born with virtue, but rather it is up to each person to acquire it through insight, constant striving, and good examples. Although there are some who by nature have much good in them, their character is an accidental one and is only a capability of attaining it. For true virtue is more foreign to our corrupt human nature than consistent with it and inherent in it. Therefore the good that a person does against his natural inclination stems, to be sure, from a propensity for virtue, but the rest comes from his temperament. The less good a person has in him naturally, the more he is obliged to follow the examples of others. If he does not do this, he acts contrary to the duties required by natural law.

I hope that the above distinction and the things derived from it will dispel the prejudices about virtuosi. It will not be so easy to generalize about all people from such poor examples, particularly since curious saints are often found in all professions, arts, and sciences, because as Horace says in *Satire* 111, Book 1: *"Delirus et Amens/Undique dicatur merito."*[49]

A good Silesian poet once intimated the following about these kinds of absurd artists and scholars: "And many a learned fool crawls with his art into a barrel,/Wanting to hatch whimsies like Diogenes in the dark." Such people have their hell on earth and consume themselves in their obscure corners all their lives. Their pleasure consists of darkness, since they flee the light like bats and night owls. They despise human society rather than being born for its pleasure. They think that other people were born into the world solely for them, whereas they too are by right obliged to serve others. Happiness for them is sought in whimsies and confused thoughts, where, on the contrary, others find unhappiness in those things and thank God they are spared such rubbish.

To be sure, it is true that sometimes tiresome and vexatious circumstances disturb everyone, especially when said circumstances are such that they are at variance with the

---

49. "He is everywhere spoken of with justice as raving and mad."

quality of moral nature. However, to oppress oneself is not only cruel, it is unjust.

I could, of course, continue this discourse on virtuosi, artists, and prejudices, and go into great detail, but I hold that what can be accomplished by means of a few things ought not to be accomplished by means of many, because it is even better to demonstrate clarity in brief. My goal has been to discuss the obligations of those who are aware that they have a special talent for one thing or another, to examine the various types of artists and virtuosi, and further to clear away all sorts of prejudices here and there so that those who as yet have no knowledge of such matters will be enlightened. Because I wish to avoid all elaborations, so as not to exceed the proper bounds of brevity, and in addition because I see such a vast field before me (particularly concerning the virtuosi and other abuses) that I would have to compose a whole treatise about them, I will leave off at this point and most sincerely wish each worthy virtuoso all that can contribute to his true happiness. I earnestly hope that those who have had no taste for fine and *galant* arts can here find instruction, and that the useless and irrational virtuosi will be helped toward reform, so that the former will prove useful to the world and the latter will not disgrace the arts.

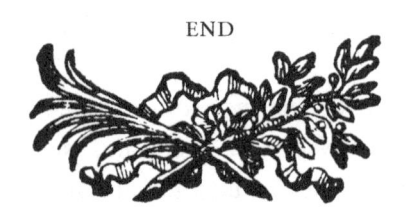

END

ENDNOTES

a. This Bonnet had not studied at a university, but rather was *ancien Paîeur des Gages du Parlement* in Paris.

b. He was formerly Captain of the Dragoons and Steward of the mother of the present King of France, but later he became Land Warfare Commissary. In 1723, before the Festival of Saint Louis, this Tillet presented the King with the painting and copper engraving of a monument. This monument is a Parnassus of metal, made for the glory of France and Louis the Great, and for the eternal memory of the famous French poets and musicians. There is space left for those of future generations as well. It is to be hoped that Germany's scholars would work not only for their bread but also occasionally for the honor of their Fatherland; thus many an artist, who does not have the opportunity of making himself generally known, would nonetheless be rescued from the corners of dark oblivion. As a result of the scholars' work, more Maecenases and patrons of the arts would pay attention to the artists. The Silesian poet [Johann Christian] Gunther, who was first published long ago, has already made a beginning and composed an excellent poem honoring the present Ducal Concertmaster of Saxe-Weimar, Pfeiffer, and had promised to immortalize more artists with his fine pen, but was taken by a very untimely death [in 1723]. This honor-loving poet gathered a large number of names of worthy people, and it is to be regretted that his noble goal was so soon interrupted.

c. *Ut quaeant laxis*
   Resonare fibris
   Mira gestorum
   Famuli tuorum,
   Solve polluti
   Labii reatum, sancte Johannes.

d. *Exercitatione* CCCII, *distinctione 7*: "*Musica Instrumenta nimis ambitiose connumeras. Quin et multa omittis, haud amissurus occasionem si ilia cognita habuisses. Misero vero existimasti fistulam aliud a syringe. Quam vocem graecam barbaro flexu in latinam deformabas. Φὸρμιγλα quoque a testudine minime sperasses: si Anacreonticam illam et Pindaricam hoc nomine ab Horatio celebratam scisses. Eandem etiam cum ipsa chely dicere instituisses: Mercurii fortuitum inventum addita Magadii arte.*"

e. *Appendix ad Censorinum*. "*Quas modulationes animadvertisse cum resonantia suavitatis in arcu sororis Apollinem tradunt et intendisse protinus citharam tum notasse quad strictiora fila in acumen excitarentur, gravibus responderent remissa. Inde fecisse tres primos modos de quibus supra dictum est. Hanc excepisse Linum, quem Apollinis tradunt filium et Nymphae Psamates (ita legit eruditissimus Cuperus) et Chrysostemidi reliquisse."*

f. *Propertius lib. 4 & 6.*
"*Non illa attulerat crines in calla solutos.*
Aut testudineae carmen inerme Lyrae."
Adde Festum Avienum.
"*Est chelys ilia dehinc, tenero qua lusit in aevo.*
Mercurius, curva religans testudine chordas.
Ut Parnassaeo munus memorabile Phoebe
Formaret nervis opifex Deus."

g. Sic Homerus loco citato.

Πῆ Εε δ' ἄρ ἐν μέτροισι ταμῶν δόγαχας χαλάμοίο,
πειρη 'νας δη νώτα διά ρινοῖο χελώνης,
Αμφι δε δερμα τανυσσε βόος παρά πιδτσιν έῇσι,
Καὶ πῃ ᾿χεις ἐνέδηχ᾽ ἐπὶ ϰ ζυγὸν ἥαρεν α᾿μφοῖν,
Εώτά ϰ συμφωνϰς οἴων ετανὺ σάίο χορδὰς.

h. *Servius ad Georg. lib 4.* "*Cum regrediens Nilus in suos meatus varia in terra reliquisset animalia, relicta etiam testudo est, quae cum putrefactaesset, et nervi ejus remansissent extenti intra corium, percussa a Mercurio sonitum dedit, ex cujus imitatione Cithara composita est.*"

i. *Jamblich. de Mysteris Aegypt. ait:* "*scriptores Aegyptios putare omnia inventa esse a Mercurio.*" *Eusebius de Praep. Evangel. lib. I, cap. 9.*

j. *Horatius carm. lib. I. Ode 10.*
"*Te canam magni Javis et deorum*
Nuntium, curvaeque lyrae parentem."

k. Sperlingi Dissertatio de Furia Sabina, p. 68, 69.

l. He says: "*Il-y-a dans le Grec* βαζδιτων: *quoique ce mot et ceux de* Κιδὰρα, Φόρμιηξ *et autres fuissent en aparence des noms d'instrumens differens.*"

m. *Alia aut ern* he says: "*Si quis curiosius inquirat inveniet instrurnenta bellica et cupiditates flarnantia vel arnores incendentia, et anirnum irarnque irritantia. In bellis itaque suis tuba utuntur Hetrusci, fistula Arcades Siculi autem instrumentis quae apellant* Πηχτίδας, *Cretenses Lyra, Lacedaemonii tibia, curnu Thraces.*" *Tyrnpano Egyptii et Arabes Cymbalo L. D., pag. 164, edit. Sylburgiana.*

n. His words read as follows: "*Caeterurn apud Graecos veteres in conviviis ad compotandurn comparatis et rotantibus poculis ad Haebraicorurn Psalmorum similitudinern, canticurn quoque apellabatur* Σχὸλιον *canebatur* cornrnuniter ornnibus voce simul prae una clarnantibus et nonnunquarn etiarn per cantici vices propinationem circurn agentibus. *Qui autem erant ex iis Musicae paulo peritiores etiarn ad Lyrarn canebant.*" pag. 165, L. D.

o. Homerus Odyss. 21. ἐυϛρεφὲς ἔντερον οἰὸς.

p. Polux L. 4, c. 9. Μὲρη καὶ τῶν ὁργανων νευραὶ, Χορδαὶ, λίνα, μὶτοι.

q. Ode LVI ad Apollinem.
*Ανά βαρϐιτὸν δονησῶ
Αεθλός μὲν γ' πρόκειται.
Μελέτη δ ἔπεϛι πάντὶ.
Σοφιῆς λαχόντ' ἄωτον.*
Which Monsieur Longepierre translates as follows:
"*Je vais jouer du Luth; non que l'on propose,
quelque prix glorieux, dont l'eclat m'y dispose.
Mais c'est que dans ce tems, tel est le docte soin,
de ceux, dont la Sagesse est dans le plus haut point.*"

r. Anacreon.
*Ιερὸν γάρ' εϛὶ Φοίϐν
Κιδάρη δ'αϕνη τρίπχς τε
Ααλέω δἔρωτα Φοίσχ,
Ανεμὠλιον τ' οἰζρον.*
Which Longepierre translates:
"*Ce laurier immortel, ce luth, ce trepied Saint, Sont sacrez au Dieu qu'honnore le Parnasse.*"

s. Horatius Ode XXXII.
"*Dic latinum barbite carmen,
Lesbio primum modulate civi.*"

t. He says: "*Organum vocabulum est generale Vasorum omnium musicorum, hoc autem cui folles adhibentur, alio Graeci nomine appellunt ut autem organum dicatur magis ea vulgaris est consuetudo Graecorum,*"

u. Titus Livius Lib. 39, Rom Hist. "*ad tertium nonas Matias Cn. Manlius Volso de Gallis qui Asiam incolunt, triumphavit, serius ei triumphandi causa fuit ne Q. Terentio Culleone Praetore causam lege Petilia diceret et incendio alieni judicii, quo L. Scipio damnatus erat, conflagraret: eo insensoribus in se quam in illum judicibus, quod disciplinam militarem severe ab eo conservatam, successor ipse omni genere licentiae corruperit. Neque ea sola infamiae erant, quae in provincia procul ab oculis facta narrabantur: Sed etiam magis quae in militibus ejus quotidie conspiciebantur. Luxuriae enim peregrinae origo ab exercitu Asiatico invecta in urbem est. Ii primum lectos aeratos, vestem stragulam praetiosam, plagulas et alia textilia, et quae tum magnificentiae lupellectilis habebantur, monipodia, et abacos Romam advexerunt: tunc psalteriae sambucistriaeque et convivalia ludionum oblectamenta addita epulis: epulae quoque ipsae et cura et sumptu majore apparari coeptae, tunc coquus, vilissimum antiquis mancipium et aestimatione et usu in pretio esse et quod ministerium fuerat ars haberi caepta. Vix tamen illa, quae tum conspiciebantur, semina erunt futurae luxuriae."*

v. *Plautus in Sticho Act 2, Scen. 3, vers. 53-57.*
"*DI. Lectos eburatos, auratos GE. Accubabo regie.*
DI. Tum Babylonica peristromata, consiliata tapetia.
Advexit nimium bonae rei GE. Herclerem gestam bene.
DI. Post, ut occepi narrare, fidicinas tibicinas.
Sambucina advertit secum forma eximia."

w. *Alex. ab Alexandro Gen. Dier. lib. 2, cap. 25.* "*Appius quoque Claudius vir triumphalis et Sabinius, M. Caecilius et Licinius Crassus optime saltare gloriae duxerunt: sicuti fidibus sonare. Discebant enim antiqui apud magistros et artifices: nam Decius Sylla optime cantasse dicitur et Cato Censorius simpliciter cantare, non servile duxit opus.*"

x. *Svetonius cap. 25.* "*Cithara autem (scil. coronam) a. Judicibus ad se delatam adoravit, ferrique ad Agusti statuam jussit.*"

y. *Bertius in Vita Boetii says:* "*Certi inter posterioris aevi scriptores Graecos pariter ac Latinos nemo fuit in omni genere sapientiae Boetio nostro par.*"

z. He says: "*Infundis lumen studiis et cedere nescis Graecorum ingeniis.*"

aa. "*Illud certe non admittendum contenderim Boiithium morte praeventum Musicam non absolvisse.*"

ab. "*Le Luth n'avoit autrefois que six rangs de cordes: mais avec le temps on y a ajoute quatre, cinc ou six autres rangs plus bas.*"

ac. "*Quum Rex Francorum convivii nostri fama pellectus a nobis citharoedum magnis precibus expetisset, sola ratione complendum esse promissimus quod te eruditionis Musicae peritum esse noveramus. Adjacet enim vobis doctum eligere, qui disciplinam ipsam in arduo collocatam potuistis attingere.*"

ad. *Horatius in lib. de Arte Poetica vers. 395.*
"*Amphion Thebanae conditor arcis*
Saxa movere sono testudinis et prece blanda
ducere quo vellet."

ae. *Horatius lib. III, Ode XI writes:*
"*Mercuri (nam te docilis magistro)*
Movit Amphion lapides canendo
Tuque testudo resonare septem callida nervis."

af. He says in the preface to his work:
"Then Coraebus put on the fifth string,
Hiachnes of Phrygia the sixth,
Terpander, after the number and character of the planets,
the seventh."

ag. de *numero septenario conf. Aulius Gellius lib. 3, cap. 10; Macrobius lib. I, de som. Scip. p. 15, edit. Aldi.*

ah. *Cornelius Nepos cap. 2, in Vit Epaminondae:* "*Nam et citharizare et cantare ad chordarum sonum doctus est a Dionysio, qui non minore fuit in musicis gloria, quam Damon aut Lamprus; quorum provulgata sunt nomina.*"

ai. *Saxo Grammaticus, lib. 12.*

aj. *Kircherus L. IX, p. 217.* "*Cur quoque satellites extra cytharae sonum stare voluerit, non vides causam, cum Musica non omnibus ut dictum est eodem modo concitandis apta sit, sed pro diversis naturarum conditionibus alius aliter movebatur.*"

ak. *Buchananus in Historia Scotica L. 17, pag. 639. dicit:* "*Erat inter aulica ministeria David quidam Rizius, Augustae Taurinorum natus, e patre homine quidem probo, sed pauperculo: ut qui elementa Musices docendo aegre se et familiam sustentabat: hic cum nullum quod suis patrimonium relinqueret, haberet, liberos utriusque sexus psallere docuit. Ex iis, cum David in adolescentiae vigore constitutus et non inamoena voce praeditus et a patre in Musicis institutus esset in spem Fortunae liberalioris erectus, Niceam in aulam Ducis Sabaudiae, nuper in suam ditionem restituti profectus est: se ibi non pro spe acceptus, cum omnium rerum egenus omnia circumspiceret, tandem in Morettium incidit, jam tum, Ducis missu iter in Scotiam adornantem. Hunc cum secutus eo venisset, nec Morettius, homo non admodum copiosus operam ejus, aut necessariam aut utilem sibi, aestimaret, ibi sustinere paulum et fortunam denuo experiri, decrivit: eo maxime adductus, quod Regina diceretur, cantionibus valde ablectari, nec ipsa Musices, omnino imperita esset, Igitur, ut primum sibi aditum ad eam patefaceret, egit cum cantoribus, quorum plerique Galli erant, ut inter eos appareret: semel atque iterum auditus placuit, statimque in eorum collegium adscriptus est:*" etc.

al. I have indicated this carefully because many countries were called by this name, and because Besard calls him a "*Venedum.*" Thus it is uncertain where he was active.

am. "*Anglia Dulandi Lacrymis moveatur:
Hoberti Julia se jactet terra superba chely.*"

> *Geldria Rhedani, Diomedis sarmata tollat*
> *vel Laurenzini carmine Roma caput.*
> *Aurea Parisios oblectet Musa Camilli*
> *Drusinosque vehat Misnis ad astra suos.*
> *Phœbeum testudo melos quae percita nevos*
> *Edit, Phaheo nixa favore nitet:*
> *Nixafavore nitit Cythereidos: enthea claro*
> *Praeclaris gaudet gentibus esse loco.*
> *Ergo tuum Philgre Rudentum suspice, terris*
> *Hac notum multis carminis arte virum.*
> *Vos Nymphas Veneres testor, quibus aure canorem*
> *Arrecta toties condere cura fuit:*
> *Orphea non mollis vincit vel Ariona cantu?*
> *Non Thamyrae superat plectra melosque lyrae?*
> *Sive tono resonat Phrygio, seu Dorica vocem*
> *seu numeris nectit Lydia Musa suis?*
> *Euge novis cœptis gratatur Apollo: Camœnae*
> *Apolaudunt operi, candite Jano, tuo.*
> *Invida quod Fortuna, Themis vel diva moratur,*
> *Immortale dabit Musica culta decus."*

an. Melchior Newsidler: "Today's music can be expanded and perfected on the lute with an extra string (together with its octave) added to the previous eleven, so that a lute properly strung with thirteen strings can perfectly produce the cadences in any piece."

ao. *"Exploratus est mihi Cels. V. animus variis in me collocatis beneficiis testatus. Memini, cum hic Lipstae bonarum literarum causa versamini, non modo vos, Illustrissimi Principes, ab hoc studio non abhorruisse, sed authores etiam fuisse mihi, ut, quod nunc celsitudini vestrae offero, satagerem."* etc.

ap. He says: *"Nam et lassitudinem animi ex negotiis mitigat, et otii molestiam temporisque taedia lenit; animum etiam variorum affectuum aestu perturbatum sedat et ad rectam rationem componit."*

aq. He judges the matter as follows: *"Quod autem multi praeclara hac arte abutuntur ad Lasciviam et libidinem, commune id omnium fere artium fatum est; ideoque vel minimum propterea hujus artis usui derogari, est iniquum."* etc.

ar. He writes about it thus: *"Quin etiam me hujus instituti adeo nec poenitet nec pudet, ut etiam progressuum meorum in hoc studio documenta publica extare cupiam. Suadet id mihi Italorum, Gallorum et Germanorum quorum usus sum institutione, authoritas."*

as. *Besardus:* "*Ut de hodierna ejus, apud neotericos Musicos exercitatione et usu solerti nunc taceam: quo a doctis plerisque certatim ita colitur, et excolitur, ut ad Laudem et dignitatem ejus nil accedere posse, videatur; unde non immerito Princeps quasi, et Regina Musicorum Instrumentorum omriium Testudo appellari atque censeri ab omnibus Philomusis debet.*"

at. *Lettres sur les Anglois et Françoises, pag.104.* "*Quoioqu'il en soit et sans etre prevenu pour et contre les Francois, pour peuqu'on les connoisse on s'aperçoit aisement, qu'en estimant si fort l'Esprit, les Manieres l'Exterieur, ils negligent le solide, qu'ils attachent a la Bagatelle, et que, generalement parlant, ils ne connoissent guere le Prix des choses.*"

au. He says: "And because it just then happened that the splendid French theorbist and lutenist Monsieur de St. Luc was passing through Berlin on his way to Vienna, he was detained here until the nuptials to increase the forces of the *sinfonie,* together with the well-known artists in our service- Ricks, Attilio, Volumnier, and others."

av. "*Les luths de Bologne sont les plus estimés par la qualité du bois qui est cause qu'on en tire un plus beau son.*"

aw. "*Un Autheur digne de foi dit qu'on a vû a Paris un Luth d'or qui revenoit a 32000 ecûs.*"

ax. De *Polymathia cap. i, p.* 2. "*Ut enim ille et dives et Rex, et nobilis; ita et Sutor et Faber et Pistor sibi erat. Cujus elegans et festivum ab Apulejo in Hippia producitur exemplum: qui praeter eximiam artium omnium ingenuarum cognitionem omnium opificiorum erat callendissimus. Nam quae secum habebat, omnia sua manu consecerat, et vestes et calceos et annulum et signaculum in gemma faberrimum. Simile, imo majus in Julio Caesare Bottifanga exemplum proposuit Erythraeus Pinacoth. ii, n. 17, qui praeter singularem in omnibus artibus liberalibus peritiam femoralia, thoraces, sibi ipse formabat suebatque; Omni instrumento Musico non canebat solum egregie, sed et illa melius quam quivis alius artifex conficiebat: penicille pictores; acu pingendo Arachnen ipsam provocabat; ut mulierculis, quae artem ipsam profitebantur, pudorem incuteret.*"

ay. *Ummius in Processu pag.* 262. "*Duriuscule dictum vel scriptum non statim est injuriosum.*"

az. "*Man muss sich nicht ohnbillig verwundern, wie die sinnreiche Vernunfft nach Art der emsigen Bienen in das unachtbare hölzerne Gefässlein einen so grossen Schatz Kunst-reicher und artiger Lieblichkeit der* concordantzen *hat mögen zusammen tragen und verbergen können.*"

ba. *Maxim* XLI. "A wise man," he says, "never speaks in superlatives, for in such a manner one approaches neither wisdom or prudence. Through exaggerations *(quod bene notandum)* a man prostitutes his reputation to such an extent that the poor reason and miserable judgment of him who exaggerates are betrayed.

bb. *"Thiorba a Testudine differt, ait pag. 476, cap. 11, Kircherus quod illa duplici collo (vocamus autem collum, illam partem, intra quam verticilla chordas agglomerant) haec unico constet. Inventum Neotericorum est, cum apud antiquos nulla fiat horum Instrumentorum mentio. Thiorba nomen suum invenit a circumforanio quodam Neapolitano, qui primus Testudinis collum productius duplicavit; chordas diversas addidit, cum primum non nisi barytono serviret, atque hoc instrumentum joco quodam vocare solebat Thiorbam; vocant autem Thiorbam id instrumentum, quo chirothecarii odorifera molere solent, estque mortarium quoddam prorsus simile molulis illis, quibus amygdala, synapi alique grana insuper affuso liquore convenienti in lac dissolvere solent. Hoc instrumentum primus deinde excoluit clarissimus Hieronymus Capsperger, Nobilis Germanus, et ad eam perfectionem perduxit, ut hoc tempore merito reliquis instrumentis palmam praeripuisse videatur; cum nullum instrumentum majorem varietatem harmonicam habeat, imo solum aptum fit ad diatonico-chromatico-enharmonicam methodum exhibendam."*

bc. *loc. cit. Sciendum igitur est: "Testudinem, Mandoram, Citharam essentialiter non discrepare, sed multitudine tantum chordarum et earundem concordantiarum methodo."*

bd. loc. cit. *"Vix Musicum Philosophicum decere ad ea, quae et usu jam viluerunt, et Artificum etiam inftmae sortis"* (as the *quinterna* is used by Italian comic actors and clowns merely for strumming and fool's songs) *"propria se dimittere."*

be. *Lib. 2, Historiarum: "Vitia magia amicorum quam virtutes dissimulans."*

bf. *Dissert. proemial. sens. Ver. et Fals. pag. 10, par. 25. "Contrarium vero testudine scienter ludentium digitorum argutiae evincunt."*

bg. It is called *chanterelle* from [the French verb] *chanter*, to sing, because it contributes the most to the melody.

bh. "The system of five lines," he says, "(the lutenists will not take it amiss if I argue inductively and omit their six lines)..." NB [Baron's note] Very shrewd; we will worry a great deal about it.

bi. *Li b. V. de natura rerum* or *T. II, pag. m. 334, seqq. Edit. Paris, Anno 1692.*

bj. *Lettres sur les Anglois & François, pag. 58. "Les Italiens, situez dans un pais delicieux, ont pris pour eux les delices, l'art de contenter les sens et ils y ont si bien reuissi qu'ils sont devenu entierement sensuel c'est a dire des gens chez qui dans le general il ne faut pas chercher de raison."*

bk. *loc. cit.* "*Les Allemands renomez de tout tems pour les Avantages du Corps, tournent leurs plus grand soin a le bien former, s'atachent aus Exercices et la Parure et croient ne pas negliger l'Esprit quand ils etudient les Langues et les Sciences telles qu'on les en seigne dans les Ecoles: dela leur Raison ne sçauroit s'entendre aussi loin qu'elle iroit sans cela.*

bl. Christoph. Laurent. Bilderbeck in the *Teutscher Reichs-Staat, Part. I, cap. 2, pag. 18.* "The Germans have one principal flaw, namely the too-great desire to see foreign countries and to swing their patrimony, or at least for a few years their incomes, to foreign nations, to use foreign fashions, manners, and customs, and conversely, to reject and be contemptuous of all that reeks and smacks of old German fashion, tradition, and honorable old German customs."

bm. *Du Loir Voyage du Levant, pag. 173.* "*Les Turcs quand ils mangent ont des Musiciens a leurs mode qui craillent et qui hurlent plus tot qu'ils ne chantent et bien qu'ils se vantent de pratiquer aussi bien que nous les douzes modes de la Musique ils ne scavent point faire d'autres accords que l'octave s'il ce n'est qu'en touchant, ils en rencontrent quelques autres per hazard et jamais par recherche.*"

bn. "*Abdelmoumen est le plus celebre Musicien Persan de l'Antiquité qui a compose une infinite d'Ouvrage. C'etoit le Lully de son tems.*"

bo. *Guido Pancirollus de Reb. deper. & nov. invent.* "*Nam ut Aristophanes Autor est, per Citharae callentem, Veteribus homo sapiens et gratiis omnibus ornatus fuit indicatus: eum contra, qui nullum Musices sensum aut gustum haberet, eundem vel insensatum esse vel spiritus discordes et invicem repugnantes habere judicarent.*"

bp. *Orchestre, Cap. II, pag. 71.* "This *basso continuo* or *bassus generalis* is an extemporaneous composition, one of the most essential elements of today's musical performance. It was invented or developed about the year 1600 by an Italian named Ludovico Viadana, who wrote the first treatise on the subject."

bq. *Guido Pancirollus de Charact. literar.* "*At hodie eo deventum est, ut Nobilium natio indecoram esse literarum, cognitionem claris penatibus ortis existimet: dum res consentaneae et mutua ope connexae, Generis claritas et literarum peritia, collidi inter se et dissidere putantur, quo errore factum, ut disciplinae olim ingenuae appellatae, ad plebem jam diu transierint, non tantum a Nobilibus sed etiam (o mores perditos!) a sacricolis repudiatae: ne non satis generosus esse ordo Antistitum et praesulum putaretur.*"

br. "*Data scilicet est Musica hominibus tanquam lac animae, et gratissimum solicitudinis lenimentum, et laborum solatium atque remedium ad inducendam humanarum clamitatum oblivionem, quibus vita haec nostra undique septa deprehenditur.*" Guido Pancirollus de Musica.

bs. *Segm.* 27. *vel Guido Panciroll.* "*Diogenes Cynicus carpere solebat Musicos: qui cum Lyrae chordas congruenter temperarent, animi mores inconcinnos haberent.*"

INDEX

Amphion 12, 45, 180
Anacreon 25, 31, 32, 179
Apollo 21, 22, 26, 31, 32, 37, 53, 95, 182
Aristophanes 153, 185
Bocheron 7
Boethius 19, 39, 40, 41, 74, 105
Camillus 51
Censorinus 22
Chitarrone 51
Chorton 94
Cicero 107
Cithara 178, 180
Cittern 26
Clavichord 90, 103, 106, 138
Clemens Alexandrinus 25, 26
Clodovaeus 41
Colascione 104, 107
Consonance 86
Cortaro, Antonio 78
Dacier, Madame 31, 32
Denss, Adrian 135
Dentice, Fabritio 60
Descartes, Rene 5, 91
de Vaumeny 60
Diogenes 6, 107, 166, 167, 171, 174, 175, 186
Dissonance 86
Dix, Aureus 66
Dlugorai, Adalbert 60
Doctrine of the affections iv
Douth, Robert 48
Dowland, John x, 50, 60
Dowland, Robert 60

Dufaut 72
Eckstein, Antonius 65, 66
Edinthonius, Johannes 60
Edlinger, Joseph 80
Emotions 48, 67, 113
English, lute treatises of i
Enlightenment iii, v
Epp, Matthaeus 79
Erasmus of Rotterdam 93
Fantasia vi, 150
Ferrabosco, Alfonso 59, 60
Festus Avienus 22
Fichtholdt, Hans 78
Fingering 116
Fleury, Nicolasi i
Flute vi, 6, 71
Forqueray, Antoine 71
Francisque, Antoine 135
Frederick the Great vi
French i, ii, iii, iv, v, vi, ix, x, 9, 16, 20, 41, 42, 54, 55, 56, 62, 64, 65, 70, 71, 72, 75, 85, 98, 145, 177, 183, 184
Frey, Hans iii, 77
Fuhrmann, Georg Leopold 135
Fux, Matthaeus 79
Gafurius, Franchino 15
Gallot, Jacques 16, 72
Gaultier, Denis? 71
Gaultier, Ennemond i
Georgius, Joachim 135
Gerle, Hans 56, 57
Germans, lute treatises of i

Gleim, Johann Laurentius 69
Gleitsmann, Paul 70
Gracian y Morales, Baltasar 109
Graun, Carl Heinrich ix
Grave 70
Greeks 6, 22, 26, 32, 34, 37, 38, 40
Greff-Bakfark, Valentin 60
Guitar 31, 40, 41, 73, 105
Güttler, Johann Michael 80
Handel, George Frederick 90
Harp 22, 26, 37, 103, 104
Hartung, Michael 77, 78, 79
Haussler 65
Heinichen, Johann iv, 157
Heliogabalus 37, 38
Henry, Lord Darnley 49
Hesse 71
Hinterleithner, Ferdinand Ignaz vi, 65
Hoffmann, Johann Christian 79, 177
Hoffmann, Martin 79
Homer 12, 22, 26
Horace 12, 21, 23, 32, 33, 45, 63, 85, 114, 175
Hove, Joachim van den 135
Huelse, Achatius Casimir 64, 65
Hummel, Matthaeus 80
Hunichius, M. Christoph 51, 59
Huwet, Gregory 50
Isidore 33, 37, 38
Jacobi 69
Jamblichus 23
Johann Anton 64
Juvenal 33

Kammerton 94
Kapsberger, Hieronymus 105
Keyboard 19, 56, 98, 101, 102, 103, 104, 147, 156, 157
Kircher, Pater Anastasius ix, 7, 43, 47, 48, 104, 105, 113, 164
Kropfganss, Johann 115
Kuhnel, Johann Michael the Elder 69
Lampridius 37
Lamprus 46, 181
Lauffensteiner, Wolff Jakob 65
Laurencini 19, 50, 60
Leibnitz 8
Leopold I 64, 164
Longepierre 25, 31, 179
Losy von Losynthal, Count 63, 64, 80, 95
Louis XIII 164
Lully, Jean Baptiste 71, 145, 153, 185
Lyre 22, 23, 25, 26, 33, 37
Mace, Thomas i
Machul 44
Maler, Lucas iii, 51, 77
Mandora 105
Marais, Marin 71
Mary, Queen of Scots 49
Mattheson, Johann iii, iv, ix, 7, 68, 73, 83, 84, 85, 86, 88, 89, 90, 91, 92, 93, 94, 95, 96, 98, 102, 103, 104, 105, 106, 107, 116, 118, 124, 155
Meley 66
Memorization 134

Mendel, Arthur 94
Mercure 60
Mercury 21, 22, 23, 26, 37, 45
Mertel, Elias 60, 135
Mest, Raphael 77
Meusel viii, 68
Minnin 44
Moliere 86
Montbuysson, Victor de 60
Mouton, Charles i, 16, 56, 72
Nero 23, 31, 37
Newsidler, Hans 51, 53, 77
Newsidler, Melchior des Noyers 53
Oboe 71
Ochsenkuhn, Sebastian ii, 18, 45, 53, 55, 56, 91
Ornaments 137
Orpheus 45, 62
Ovid 72
Pancirollus, Guido 185, 186
Pandura, Pandora. See Mandora
Perault 7, 70, 71
Pereira, Gomesio 6
Perichon, Jean 60
Perla, Hortensius 60
Petit, Monsieur 68
Petrarch 72
Pierce, Jane 57
Pindar 46
Plato 10, 36, 45, 46
Plautus 36, 180
Plutarch 46
Pohlmann, Ernst 51, 62
Pommersbach, Clayss von 77
Pomponius 60
Poulton, Diana 50

Praetorius, Michael 15, 17, 40, 63, 155, 156, 161
Prelude vi, 149
Propertius 22, 178
Puffendorff, Herr von 41
Pythagoras 12, 37
Questenberg, Johann Adam von 66
Quintilian 12
Rael, Cydriac 60
Rauch, Sebastian 80
Rausgler, Sebastian 78
Reusner, Esaias 62
Reymann, Matthaeus 135
Reys, Jakob 50, 60
Rhetoric 88, 113
Riwitzky 65
Rizzio, David 49, 50, 59
Rochi, Christofilo 78
Rochi, Sebastian 78
Rude, Johannes 51, 58, 59
Rüdiger, Andreas 1, 110
Sage de Richee, Philipp Franz le 16, 156
Saint-Luc, Jacques de 72
Scaliger, Joseph 18
Scaliger, Julius Caesar 22, 38, 94
Schaffnitz 65
Schelle, Sebastian iii, 80
Schlinsky 65
Schmid, lute maker 79
Schmidt, Melchior 57
Schott, Martin 80
Sella alla Stella, Georg 78
Servius 23, 178
Sibborim, Rabbi Scilte 44
Sperling, Otto 23
Strings ii, 13, 22, 23, 26, 35,

36, 37, 40, 45, 51, 53, 54, 76, 79, 83, 92, 93, 94, 104, 105, 106, 107, 117, 118, 124, 129, 132, 145, 167, 182
Suite vi
Svetonius 37, 180
Tablature ii, 116, 118
Tacitus 84, 95, 107, 170
Theodoric, King 40, 41
Theorbo i, viii, 40, 58, 67, 104, 105, 106
Thorough bass 67
Tieffenbrucker, family iii
Tieffenbrucker, Leonhard 79
Tieffenbrucker, Vendelino 78, 79
Tielke, Joachim iii, 79
Tillet, Herr von 9, 177
Til, Salomon von 16, 21, 25, 38
Transcription 108
Trevoux, Society of 18, 40, 74, 76
Venere, Vendelino 78
Viadana, Ludovico 155, 156, 185
Viol i
Violin vi, 32, 33, 67, 79, 124
Virgil 12, 23
Vogel, Hans 55
Vogl, Emil 64, 66
Volso, Cnejas Manlius 34, 179
Weichenberger, Johann Georg 65
Weiss, Johann Sigismund 66
Weiss, Sylvius Leopold vi, ix, 66, 67, 68, 95, 96, 110

Welter, Johann 58
Wieland, Philipp 65

PUBLISHER'S NOTE (2ND EDITION)

The original publisher, Instrumenta Antiqua Publications (now known as Lute Stuff), thanked John Emerson and Vincent Duckles, music librarians at UC Berkeley, for their kind help and cooperation and for allowing the photography of the original German edition from their collection. The original graphic illustrations in this book come from that copy. A few of these illustrations were replaced or improved thanks to digital scans (not available at the time of the first edition).

Transcription of the musical examples were done by Stanley Buetens.

This book is printed on demand by Kindle Direct Publishing.

Made in the USA
Monee, IL
27 February 2024

54144236R00125